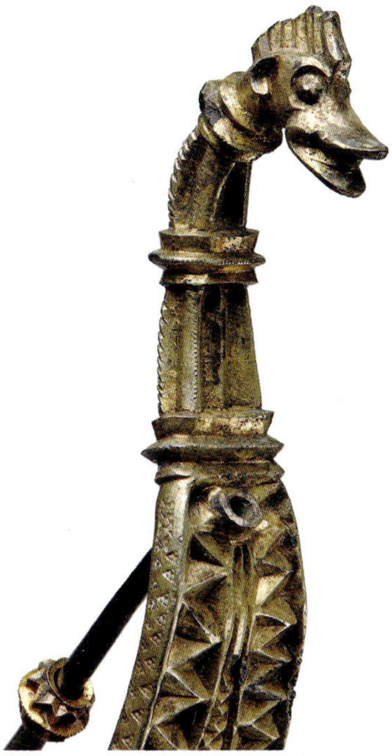

4 Who were the Vikings?

6 Origin Saga

8 From oral tradition to literature

14 Yggdrasil—connecting the Nine Worlds

22 Saga of the Journey

26 The sail made the world smaller

34 Vinland and L'Anse aux Meadows

36 Formidable warriors

42 Saga of Life

44 A hierarchical society

50 Woman in the Viking Age

52 Unparalleled artisans

56 Saga of the End of Time

58 Living among the dead

64 The end of the Viking Age

ABOVE

Large brooch with dragon head.

Gold and silver. Bornholm. 700–800 CE.
National Museum of Denmark.

FACING PAGE

Detail of a harness bow.

Bronze and gold mounted on wood.
900–1000 CE. Søllested Mark.
National Museum of Denmark.

A GREAT PEOPLE OF THE NORTH— THE VIKINGS REVEALED

The Vikings began their legendary plying of the seas and devastating raids in the 8th century. The attack in 793 on the Anglo-Saxon monastery at Lindisfarne, an important centre of Christianity, marked the start of the Viking Age, and the Vikings' reputation as ferocious warriors began to spread.

Over the next 300 years, the impacts of their trading and exploration, and their plundering and invasions, extended well beyond Europe and the Caucasus, and the edges of North America.

Their skill as sailors and expanding trade networks meant they could lay siege to major cities, as they did to Paris in 885. But by 1066, two major defeats in England marked the end of the Viking Age.

Yet if we look beyond their plundering and warfare, these Scandinavians were above all traders, farmers, talented craftspeople, and great seafarers. A people with beliefs rooted in a rich mythology and whose daily lives were inspired by superhuman destinies, glorious deaths, and destructive gods. For centuries, their mythology was transmitted orally, before being set down by Icelandic scribes in the 13th century.

Pointe-à-Callière, Montréal Archaeology and History Complex, is putting a spotlight on these fabulous Norse sagas and their material heritage with its exhibition *Vikings – Dragons of the Northern Seas*. The exhibition assembles over 650 eloquent and stunning objects from the National Museum of Denmark, which holds one of the world's finest collections of Viking artifacts. The Canadian Museum of History and The Rooms Corporation of Newfoundland and Labrador have also generously lent items for this exhibition, which also features breathtaking images from Ubisoft's video game *Assassin's Creed Valhalla*.

As you peruse this book, four spellbinding sagas will immerse you in the Viking world. The Origin Saga relates the creation of the world and Viking beliefs and cosmology; the Saga of the Journey takes you on a voyage into the vast Viking world aboard one of the period's best ships; the Saga of Life reveals the values and customs of a Norse village; and the Saga of the End of Time foretells the end of the world according to Norse mythology and relates the end of the Viking Age.

We thank MuseumsPartner in Austria, the lenders and specialists, and the entire team of partners who came together to create such a remarkable work for our visitors. *Bon voyage* on your trip into the Viking world.

Anne Élisabeth Thibault, Executive Director,
Pointe-à-Callière, Montréal Archaeology and History Complex

Rane Willerslev, Director,
National Museum of Denmark

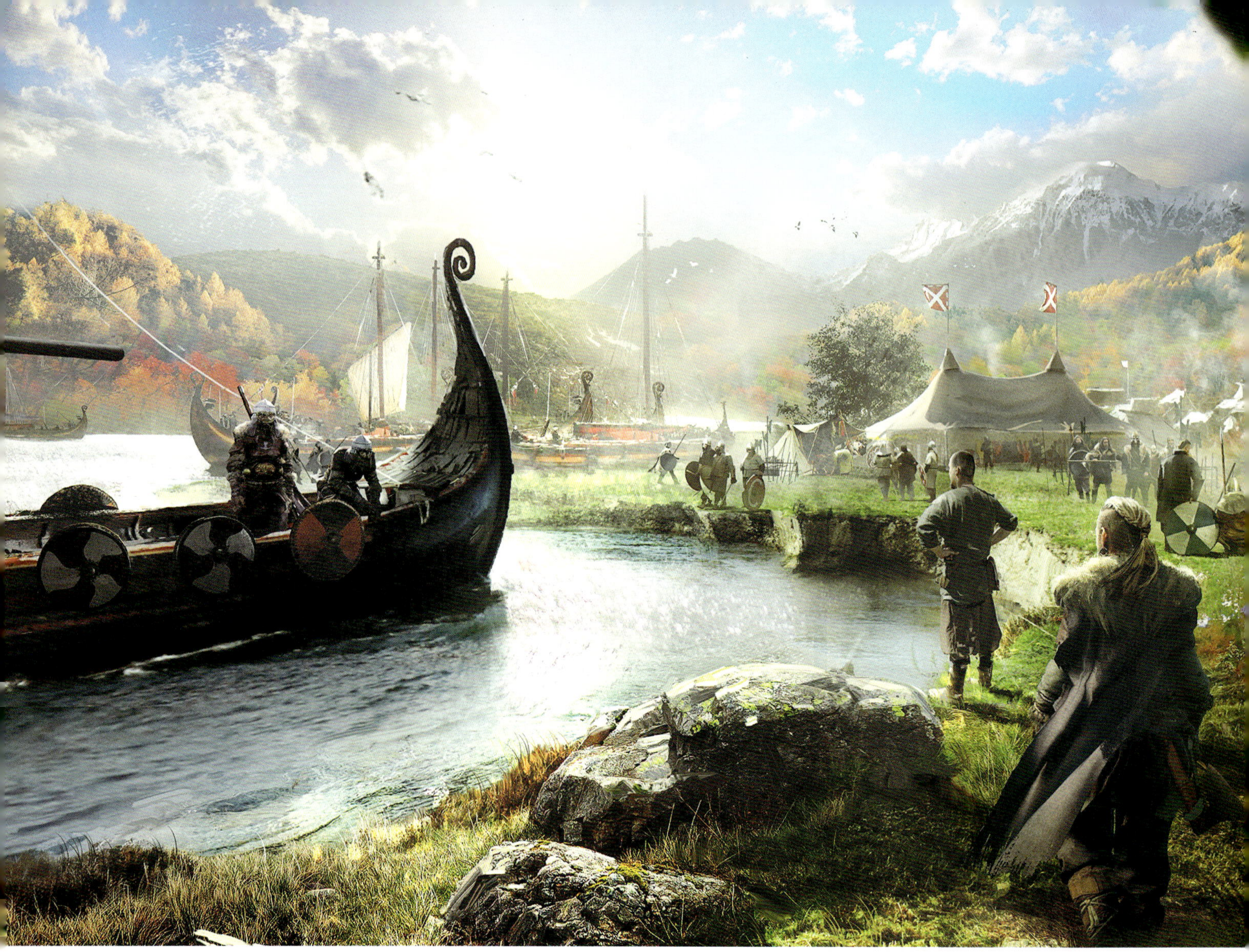

WHO WERE THE VIKINGS?

Peter Pentz, curator at the National Museum of Denmark

Vikings is the name we use to describe the people who lived in the areas where Scandinavian languages are spoken today, that is, Norway, Sweden, Denmark and Iceland. The Viking Age began sometime in the 700s and continued for the next three hundred years. The word "vikinger" (Vikings) is inscribed on a large 10th century runestone in Tirsted on Lolland, Denmark. It is also found on several other runestones, so we know that the word was used in the Viking Age. It meant "one who plunders."

When we now use the term "Vikings" to cover the entire Scandinavian population, it can be slightly confusing. Most people will associate the word "Viking" with a ravaging warrior, and not so much with the women and children of that time, and probably not at all with the substantial part of the population which were not free—the enslaved. The people who suffered under the havoc of the Vikings did not call their ravaging neighbours Vikings. The reports we have were recorded by monks and other clerics. Their descriptions of the vandals mostly emphasize that the Vikings were not Christians. The name that the authors commonly ascribe to the Vikings is "Normans," and especially, "heathens."

Our knowledge is about the Vikings comes primarily from archaeology. New finds are still being discovered; artifacts which tell us about the Vikings material world—their houses,

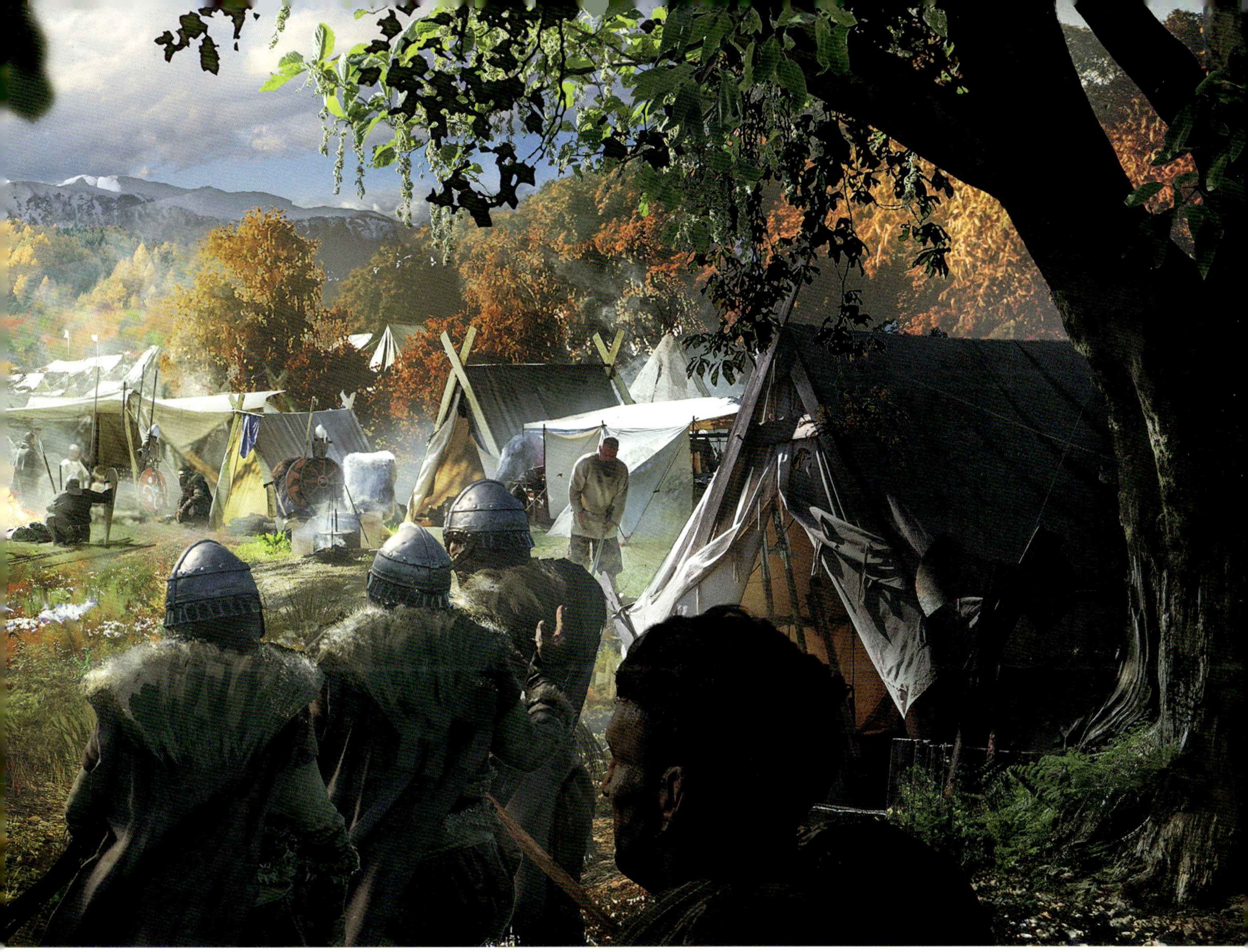

towns, ships, jewellery, tools, and much more. Archaeological finds also give us information about Vikings in a larger context—information about their way of life, economy and trade. Grave goods, images and items containing symbols give us an insight to the Vikings' thoughts, conceptual universe and imagination.

How do we discover what we know about the Vikings?

Runic inscriptions provide descriptions about families, society, journeys and language. Stories etched into the runestones are tales about fate which bring us intimately close to individual Vikings. They are condensed accounts of lives lived more than 1000 years ago. The tales are on Viking life, of women, men and children and their roles in society, their families and beliefs.

Apart from the runic inscriptions, the Vikings didn't leave us any written information about themselves. There are, however, numerous accounts from countries where the Vikings plundered and traded. The authors were mostly French, German, Irish and English chroniclers, usually monks. But travelling Arabs, Spanish, Muslims and occasionally Byzantines also contributed. All of these chroniclers had one thing in common: their accounts were from their own point of view.

The Vikings' poems and legends were recorded in the 1200s—that is a couple of centuries after the end of the Viking Age. This is also true for many of the sagas. Many of the events surely took place, but they were often altered when written down by medieval scribes. These accounts could be based on knowledge that had been handed down—that is old knowledge—but some of it could also be "fake news." In any case, sagas, poems and legends are all important sources of information about the Vikings. ▪

ABOVE

Art by Tony Zhu Shuo.

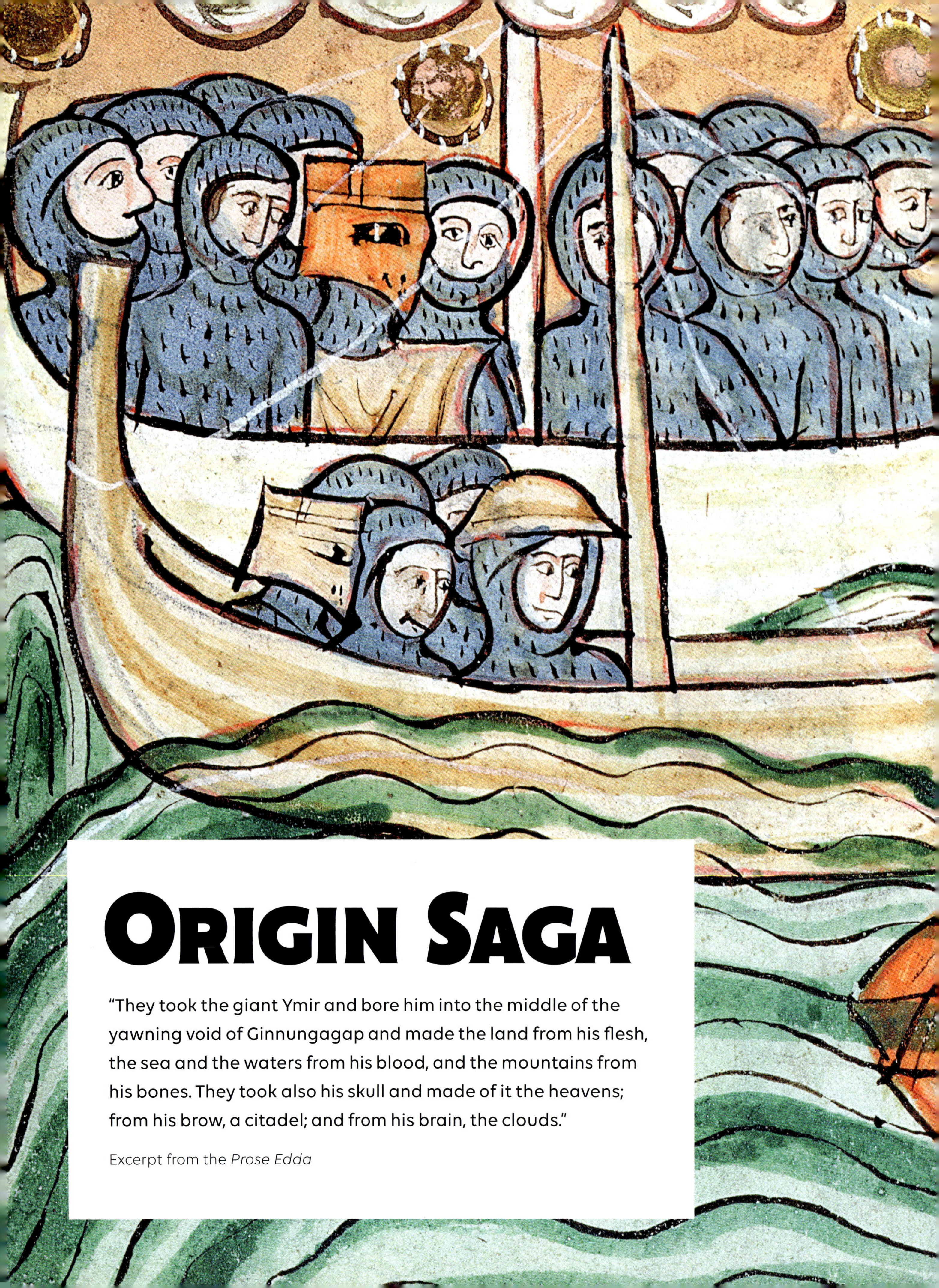

ORIGIN SAGA

“They took the giant Ymir and bore him into the middle of the yawning void of Ginnungagap and made the land from his flesh, the sea and the waters from his blood, and the mountains from his bones. They took also his skull and made of it the heavens; from his brow, a citadel; and from his brain, the clouds.”

Excerpt from the *Prose Edda*

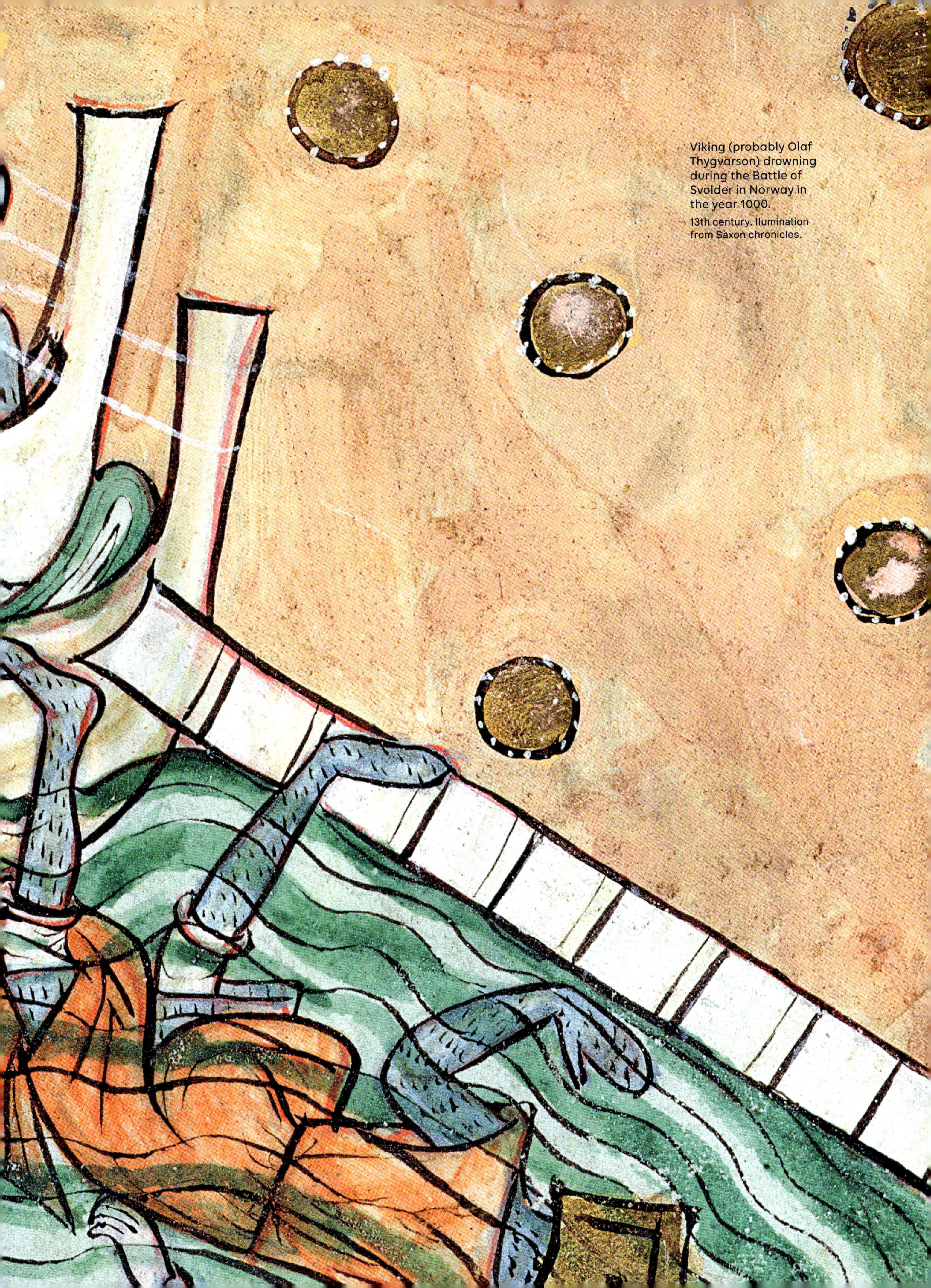

Viking (probably Olaf Thygvarson) drowning during the Battle of Svolder in Norway in the year 1000.

13th century. Illumination from Saxon chronicles.

Sagas and Skalds

FROM ORAL TRADITION TO LITERATURE

Dominique de La Tour

What we know of medieval Scandinavian literature comes from the transcription of a massive oral tradition, most of which has been lost to time. It is divided into highly metred and sonorous poetry and prose sagas, accounts that scholars have attempted to authenticate through careful genealogy.

When not sung, this oral tradition was declaimed in stentorian fashion by skalds, the Viking versions of Celtic bards. Whether itinerant or permanently in a chieftain's employ, the skald's job was to shower his benefactor with flatteries such as *drápa*, a laudatory verse form. The word *skald* stems from an Indo-European root evoking the idea of sounding or resounding; the skald was a verbal virtuoso, one who might even be tasked with engaging in delicate negotiations. Thanks to the Icelandic "lawspeaker" Snorri Sturluson (1179–1241), some of this skaldic art has been preserved.

Sturluson's opus is so colossal, it is assumed that he merely supervised a much larger compilation effort. It is best known for the *Prose Edda*, a major source of our knowledge of Norse mythology, and

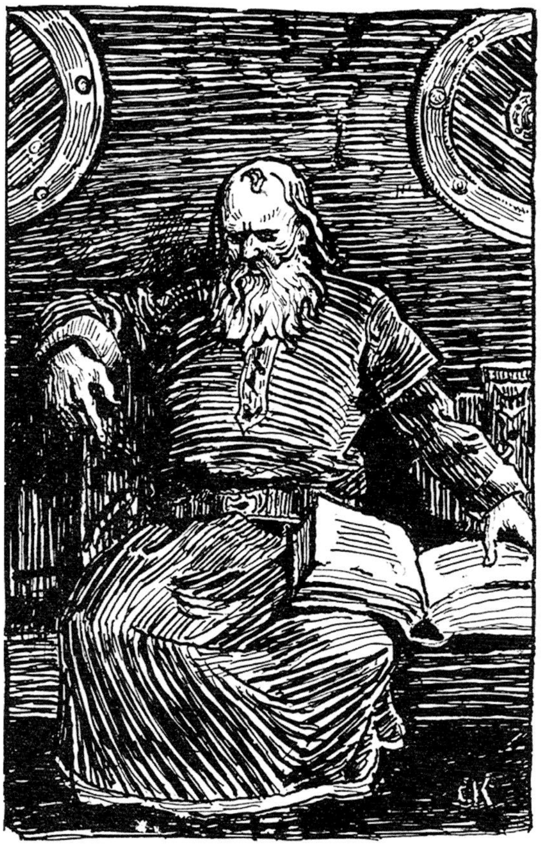

RIGHT
Snorri Sturluson
Art from 19th century.

FACING PAGE
Louis Huard
Giant Skrymir and Thor
1930. Illustration from *The Heroes of Asgard*, by par A. et E. Keary.

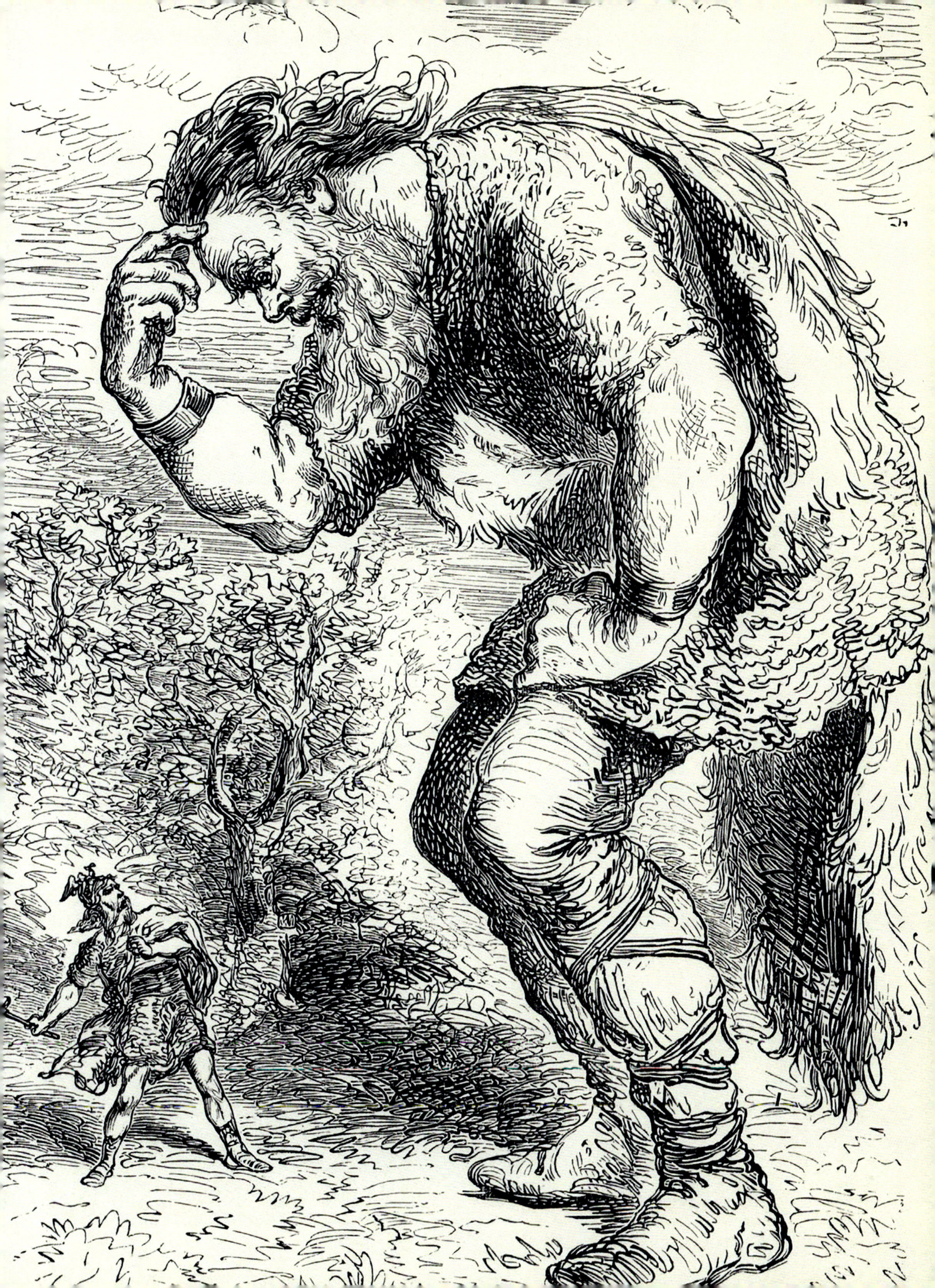

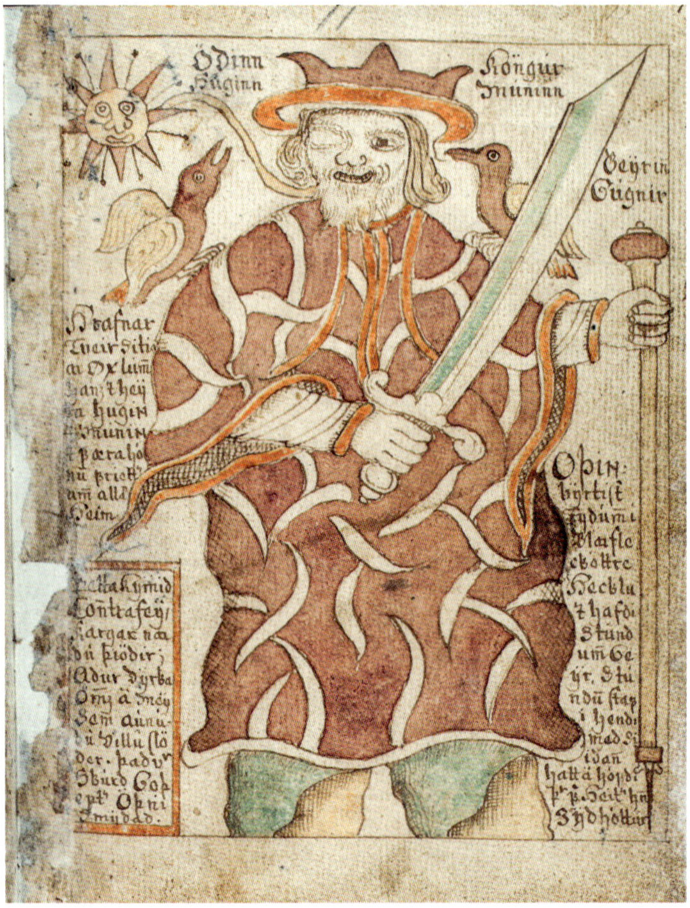

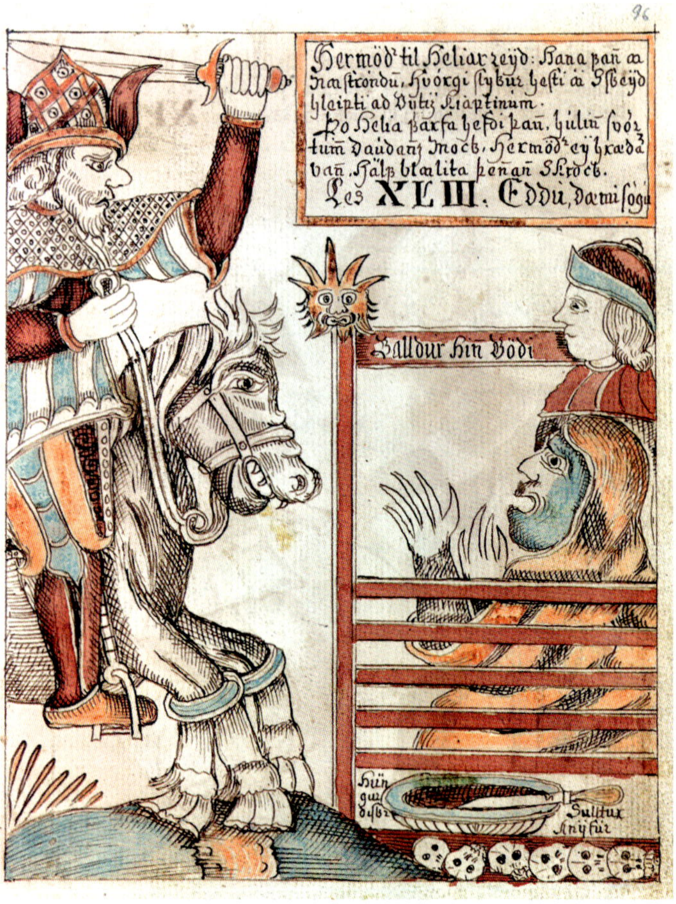

ABOVE LEFT

Odin and his ravens Huginn and Muninn, symbols of thought and mind.

ABOVE RIGHT

Hermod riding his father's famous eight-legged horse Sleipnir at the gates of Hel.

Icelandic school. 18th century. Pencil and ink on paper. Royal Danish Libarary, Copenhagen.

especially for the *Gylfaginning*, or "The Beguiling of Gylfi," a saga in dialogue. But the *Edda* also includes the *Skáldskaparmál*, or "The Language of Poetry," which names nearly 200 skalds; and the *Háttatal* ("Tally of Metres"), which lists 101 types of verse.

Sturluson's work is complemented by the *Háttalykill inn forni* ("The Old Key to Verse-forms"), which includes a *Greppamini* ("poet's reminder"), eight-line stanzas in question-response form about Norse mythology—a vital reference for the would-be skald.

But to be a skald, it was not enough to master versification and know the lives of the gods. One had to be able to use the rhetorical forms of *heiti* and *kenning*. *Heiti* ("names") is a poetic synonym, such as "steed" for a horse, or "brand" for sword. A *kenning* ("mark of recognition") is a circumlocution, such as "sea-steed" for ship, "whale's way" for the sea, or "battle-sweat" for blood. *Kennings* frequently alluded to legendary events, so "Hrungnir's slayer" referred to Mjölnir, Thor's hammer, which he used to kill the giant Hrungnir.

In scaldic rhetoric, "sea-steed" meant ship, "whale's way" meant the sea, and "battle sweat" meant blood

The earliest written transcriptions of the Norse oral tradition date from the 10th century, as the Viking Age was on the wane and Christianization was beginning, and as the memory of the poems and skaldic memorization techniques started showing cracks. The works that have come down to us were thus already somewhat degraded.

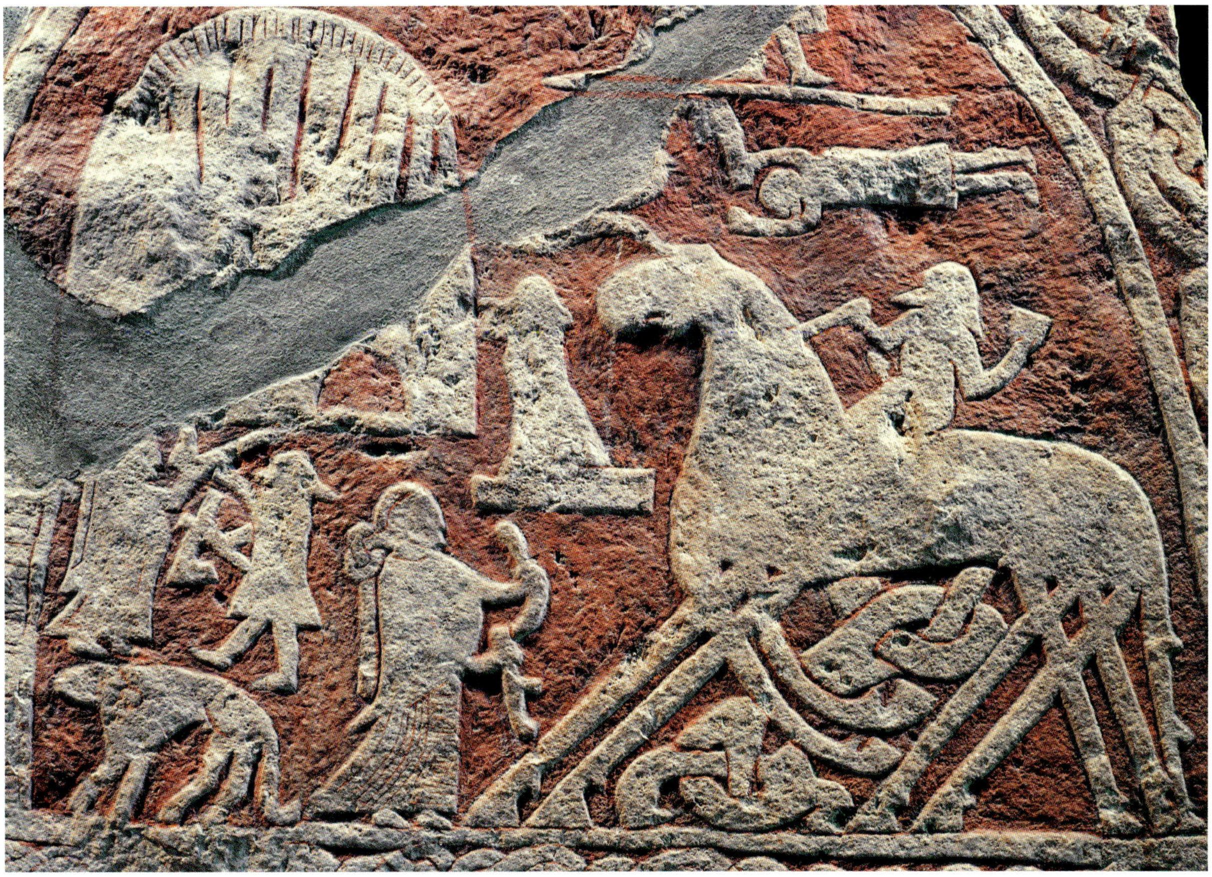

Detail of figures illustrating a saga from the Isle of Gotland.
Engraved and painted stone. 9th century. Stockholm History Museum.

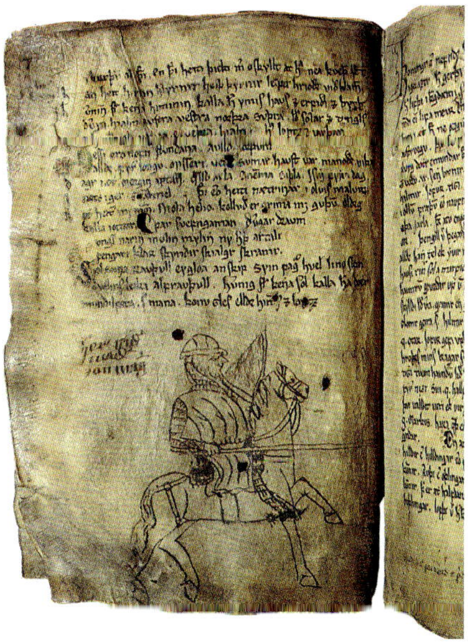

ABOVE
An knight in armour.
Page from a manuscript mentioning the *Prose Edda*. 14th century.

From Saint Olaf to Led Zeppelin

While all civilizations have been able to transmit sacred texts over several generations with a surprising degree of accuracy, Viking skalds never had a reverent respect for the verses handed down to them; it was appealing to add personal touches or even make cuts to texts deemed overly long. With the transcription of these works coinciding with the beginnings of Christianization, a not-so-subtle co-opting occurred: Adam and Eve unabashedly rubbed shoulders with Odin; the unlucky god of light, Baldr, was tacitly compared to Jesus; and to fit into biblical dualism, the ambivalent figure of Loki was quickly equated with Satan. A new genre appeared, its Latin influences extending even to its name, the *ríma*, which marked the swan song of the saga tradition.

In addition to the 18th-century Romantics who rediscovered them, these ancient Norse poems and their strict metre were influential on the likes of Swedish writer August Strindberg, American poet Ezra Pound, and Columbian novelist Gabriel García Márquez. Skaldic works would also inspire geniuses as diverse as Walter Scott, Richard Wagner, and J.R.R. Tolkien; more recent examples include English bands like Led Zeppelin (*Immigrant Song*, 1970), the Dutch founder of Viking rock, Gealdýr (writing songs in Old Norse), and the Norwegian band Ragnarök. ■

Mortal gods

Dominique de La Tour

Our knowledge of Norse gods comes primarily from the writings of Snorri Sturluson. Scandinavians worshiped two pantheons: an elite class called the Æsir, and the Vanir, who were closer to humans and their activities. These two pantheons ultimately merged. Norse gods embody constantly clashing forces in the Viking world. Like the Ancient Greek and Roman gods, the Norse gods are temperamental beings who do not always act benevolently or fairly. Their favour must be earned through sacrifice, prayer, and invocations, and they can even be compelled through magic spells. Uniquely, these gods are mortal and will be killed during a series of events foretold in Norse mythology describing the end of the world: Ragnarök.

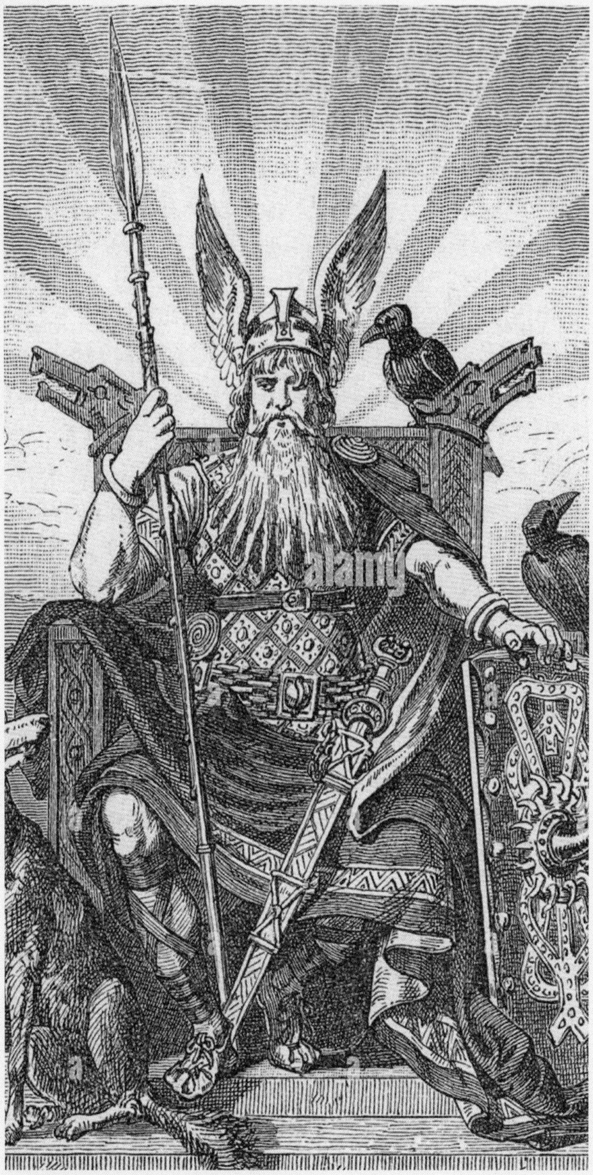

Odin (Wotan, Ygg)
Creator of the world

Odin is the "father of all" and the most feared of the gods (Wotan means "lord of frenzy"). After hanging, head down, from the sacred tree Yggdrasil for nine nights and sacrificing an eye (monocular vision was a sign of accurate sight and clairvoyance), Odin learned the power of the runes in order to predict the future. Wise, a great traveller, shrewd, and fond of wearing disguises, Odin has been compared to the Roman god Mercury. He embodies intellectual strength.

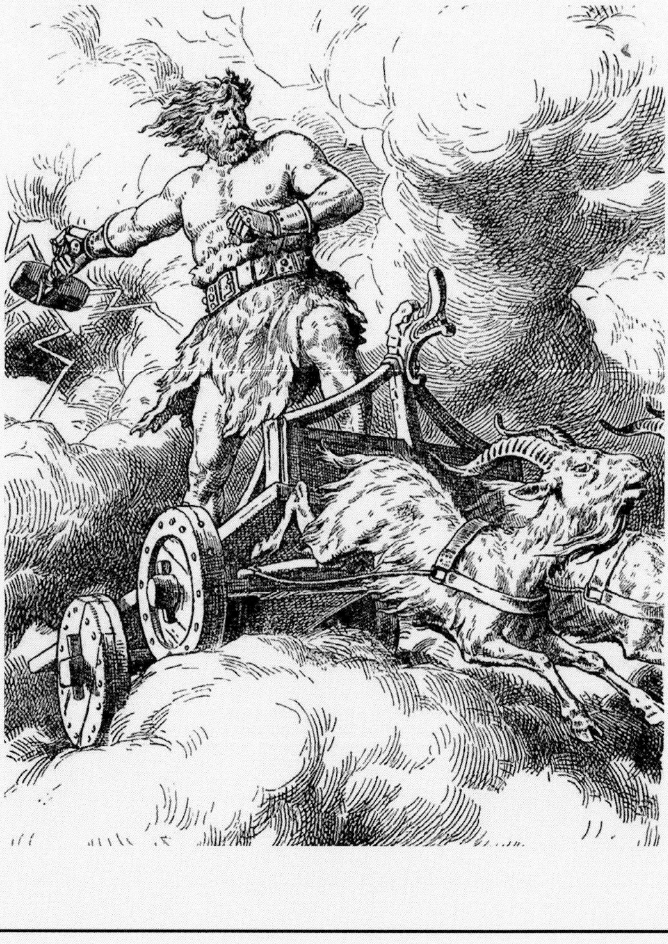

Thor
"Friend of man"

Master of lightning, which springs from his hammer, Mjölnir ("that which grinds into powder"), Thor is clearly analogous to Jupiter. Of all the Scandinavian toponyms that incorporate a god's name, one quarter invoke Thor. He was often depicted on the central pillar of homes. Holding the reins of a chariot drawn by two goats, Thor embodies physical strength.

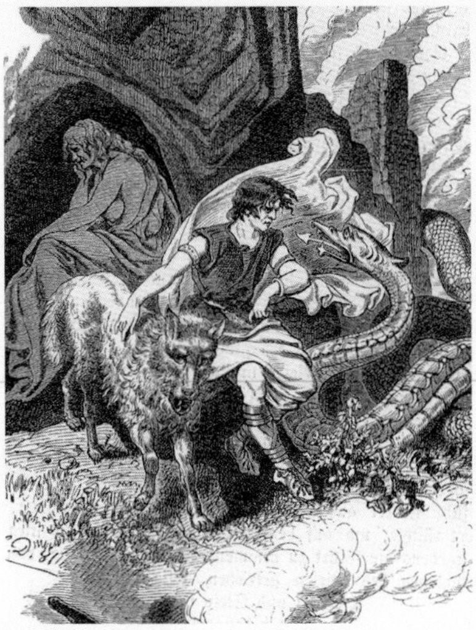

Loki
The trickster

He gave birth to Odin's eight-legged horse Sleipnir and the wolf Fenrir, who is foretold to kill Odin. Loki gained admission to the Æsir through trickery, and he has a front-row seat to make mischief and cause the Æsir harm while waiting for Ragnarök to eliminate them. Loki is a counterforce in the divine world. He embodies the evil force of trickery.

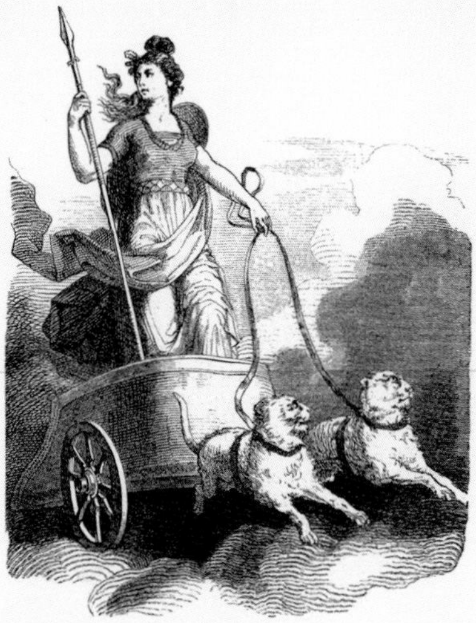

Freyja
Goddess of love

One of the Vanir, Freyja is the daughter of Njörd, god of the oceans and is the twin of Freyr. She is often represented wearing a gold and amber neck ring that gives her an irresistible charm. She also possesses a cloak of falcon feathers and rides a chariot drawn by two blue cats. She is considered the goddess of beauty and fertility but, since she welcomes warriors slain in battle, she is also associated with war.

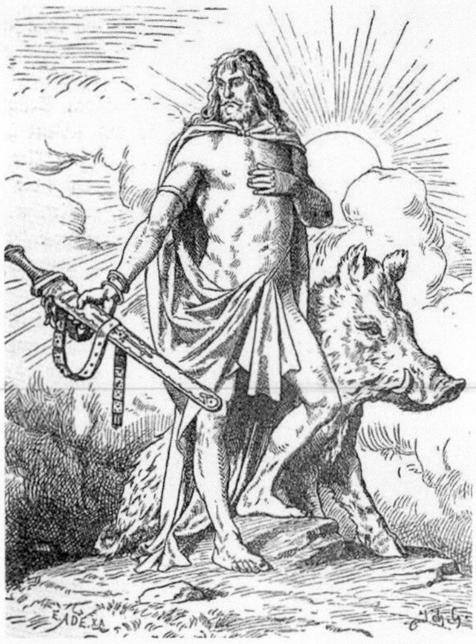

Freyr
Weather God

Freya's twin brother, Freyr is a weather god, master of sunshine and heavy rains. Along with his sister, he is one of the Vanir. He is flanked by a boar and travels on a ship that can sail on both land and water. He possesses a sword that can fight on its own. Freyr symbolizes the force of nature.

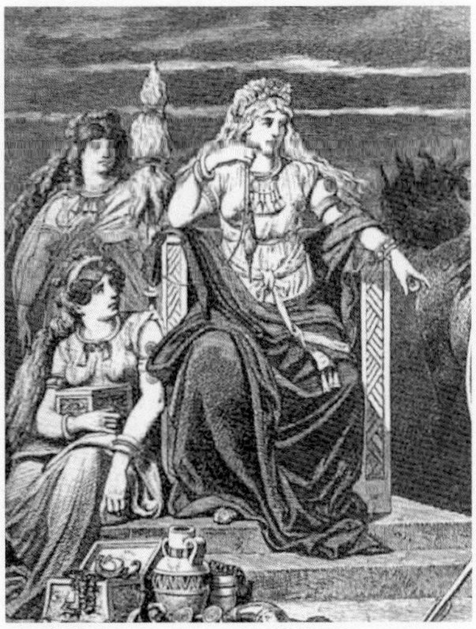

Frigg
Goddess of the household

Queen of the Æsir, Frigg is the goddess of the household, though she has an amorous and even erotic dimension. Like her husband, she has the gift of clairvoyance. Frigg leads the Valkyries, divine warriors who divide the heroes slain in battle into the hosts of either Frigg or Odin. While she symbolizes marriage, Frigg was not always faithful to her often-absent husband. She is often represented spinning with a spinning wheel.

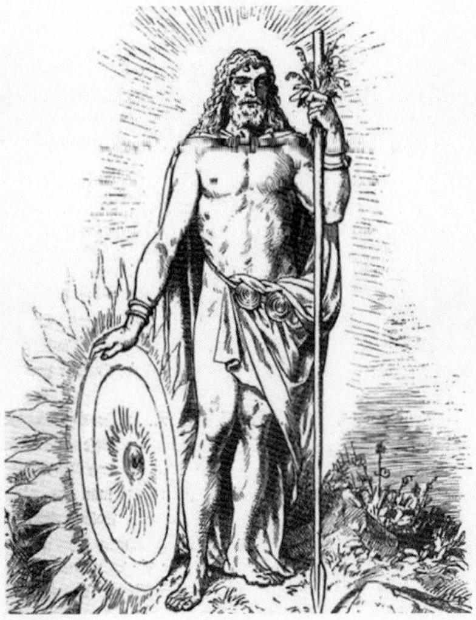

Baldr
God of light

The son of Frigg and Odin, Baldr's tragic fate is to never have any of his wishes fulfilled. His early, human-like, death prior to Ragnarök lends credence to the hypothesis that he is more a demigod, like Hercules, than a full-fledged god. He has been compared to Apollo and, later, to Jesus. He embodies the cyclic force of the seasons.

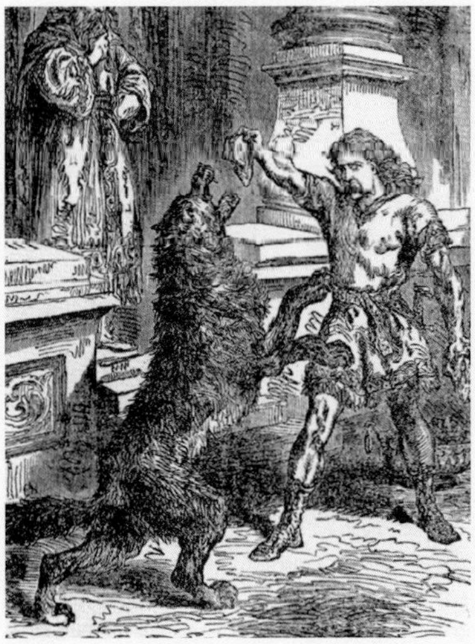

Tyr
God of righteous war

Symbolized by a stylized spear-shaped rune, Tyr is invoked to achieve victory in battle. He is also called upon as a witness in assemblies of Norse chieftains and when swearing oaths. Tyr only has one hand, the other having been bitten off by the wolf Fenrir. He symbolizes the power of stubbornness.

The above images are 19th- and 20th-century interpretations.

Home to gods, monsters, and people

YGGDRASIL—CONNECTING THE NINE WORLDS

Dominique de La Tour

Viking cosmology revolved around a tree shared among humans, monsters, and gods who were distinctly mortal.

Based on ancient sources, the world tree **Yggdrasil** is an ash or occasionally a yew. Neither species is a random choice. Both ash and yew are strong and flexible and are favourite woods among Norse peoples, who use them to make bows and spears.

Unsettling wildlife

Yggdrasil means "horse (*drasil*) of Terrible One (*Ygg*)," one of **Odin**'s many names. It is an allusion to the trance Odin enters when he hangs himself, head down, for nine days and nights—"sacrificing myself to myself"—to learn the secret of the runes.

Yggdrasil's branches rise infinitely into the heavens, and its three roots draw from three springs, including the **Mímisbrunnr**, guarded by the giant **Mímir**. In exchange for one of his eyes, Odin gains permission from Mímir to drink from its waters. As soon as he drinks, the one-eyed god, as he is henceforth called, gains access to knowledge.

Various animals live on Yggdrasil: four stags graze on its foliage, under the disapproving eye of the terrible eagle **Hræsvelgr**, which generates the earth's winds with each wingbeat. Under the ground crawls **Nidhögg**, a snake that gnaws at the tree's roots. And running up and down the tree, the squirrel **Ratatoskr** serves as a courier for the eagle and the snake as they exchange threats and taunts.

Watched over by Heimdall

Despite these injuries, Yggdrasil remains the backbone and framework of the Nine Worlds. At the very top, perched on its crown like a nest, is **Asgard,** "enclosure of the Æsir." Gods of the upper pantheon, the Æsir are ruled by Odin, who holds feasts illuminated only by sword-gleam. Worthy warriors are also invited to these feasts in Odin's palace, named **Valhalla**—hall of the val (*slain*)—and brought there by armed horsewomen called **Valkyries.** Taking the form of Odin's ravens, the Valkyries choose the warriors who have died with courage on the battlefield.

Opposite Asgard, **Helheim** is the "realm of Hel," which is found under the earth. Hel is also the name of the goddess who presides over the place. Hel comes from a root word

FACING PAGE

Art by Gilles Beloeil.

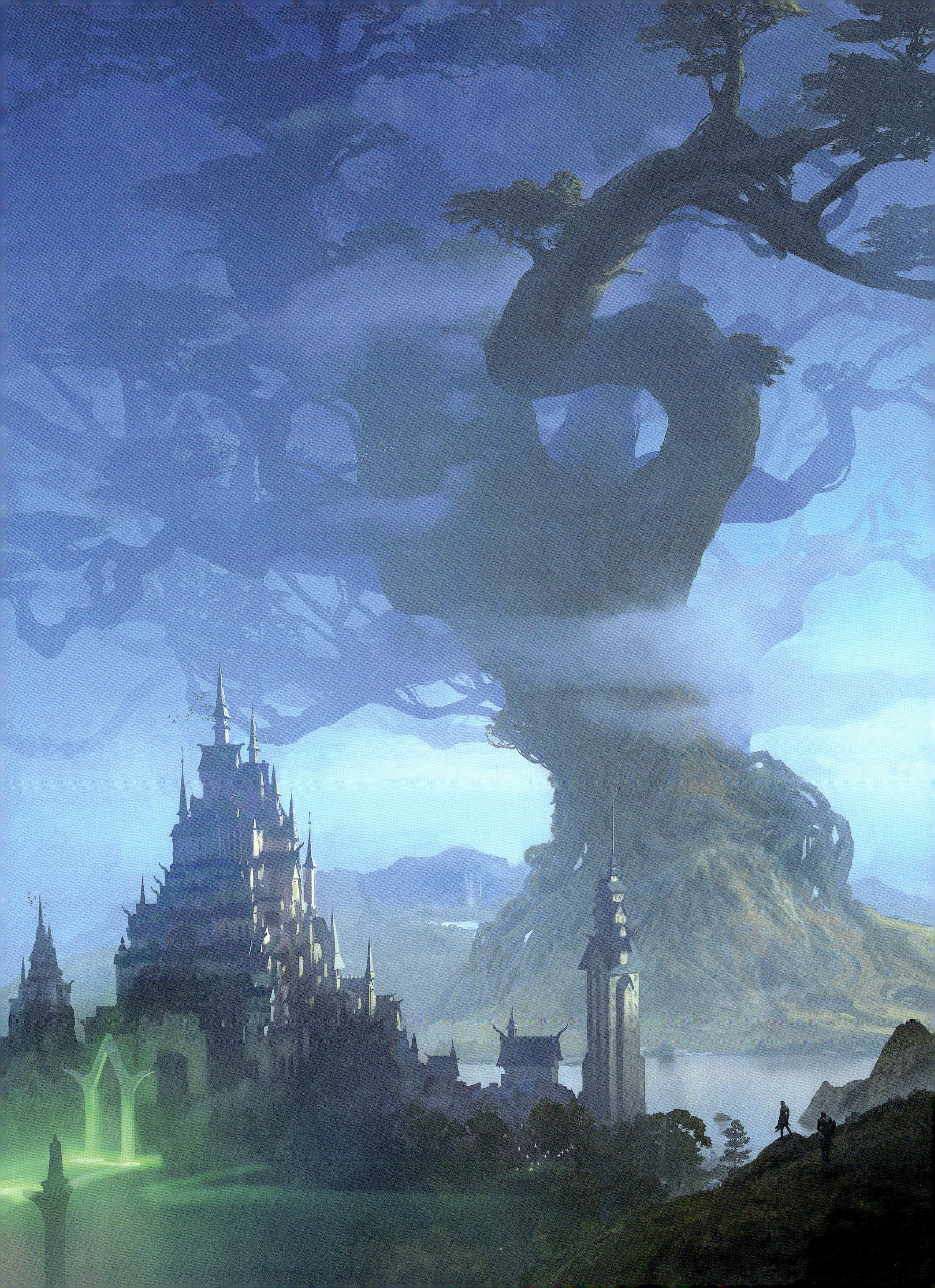

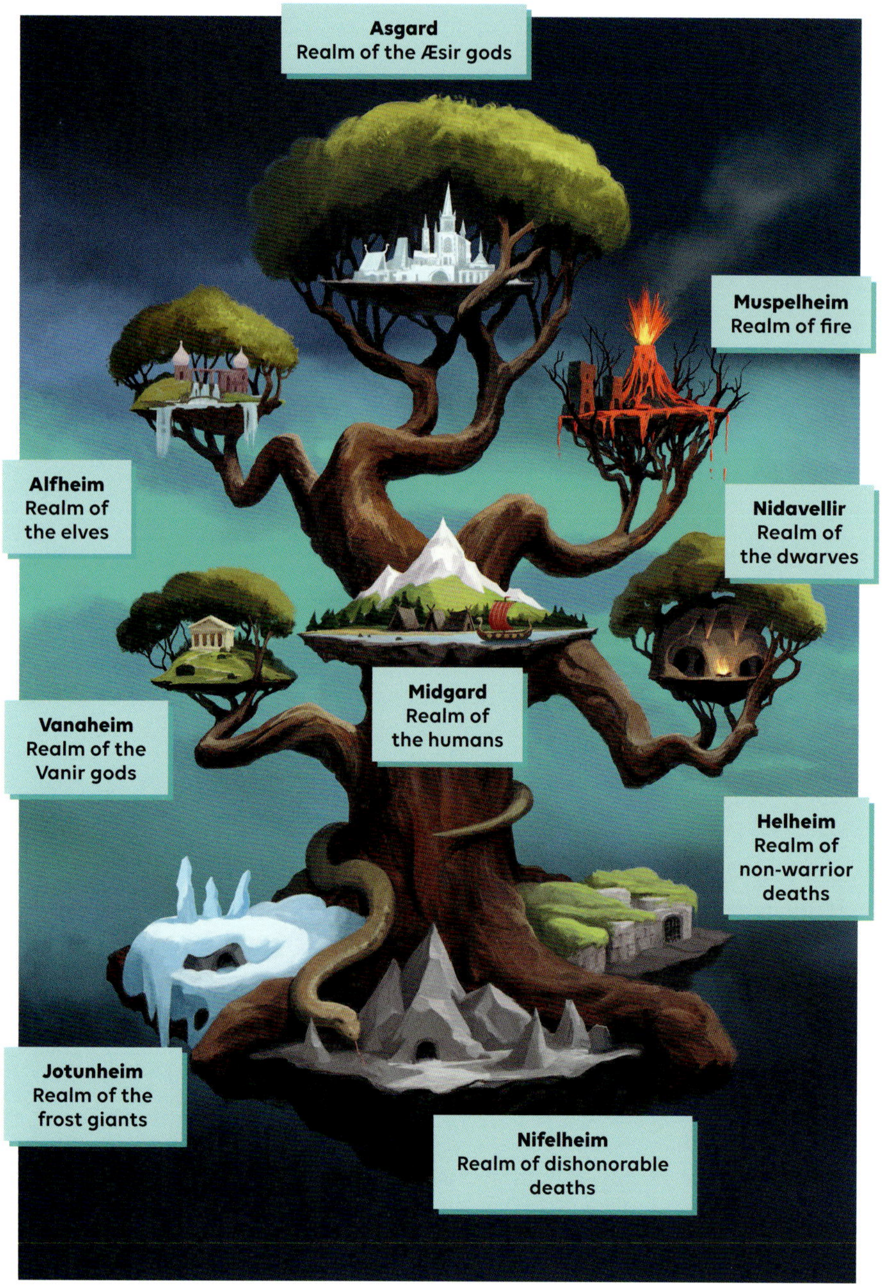

ABOVE
The Nine Worlds supported by Yggdrasil.
Illustration by Nicolas Demers. Pointe-à-Callière.

At the very top, perched on its crown like a nest, is Asgard, "enclosure" of the Æsir

meaning "conceal, hide." This is where the ordinary dead reside—those who have not died in battle. And Hel is, of course, the origin of the English word "hell."

Between the two worlds is the world of humans, **Midgard**, or "middle enclosure," located halfway up the tree trunk. Midgard is connected to Asgard by the **Bifrost**, a celestial rainbow bridge used by the gods to cross over and hold their councils. The god **Heimdall** guards the bridge, standing ready to sound the alarm on his famous horn and defend it with his sword.

Awaiting Ragnarök

Yggdrasil also supports other important spaces. **Jötunheim**, "realm of the Jötun," is a world of frost. Jötun (pl. *Jötnar*) is often translated as "giant." The word, which has the same root as the English verb "to eat," means "devour." They threaten the Æsir, symbolizing hostile forces of nature, and will emerge triumphant during Ragnarök.

Opposite the world of frost is **Muspelheim**, the world of fire. The name appears to derive from *mund spill*, or "destroyer of the world." Muspelheim is guarded by the giant Surtr, who will destroy the Nine Worlds during Ragnarök.

Tree worship

A yew still stood in front of the temple dedicated to the Norse gods in Uppsala, Sweden as late as the 11th century. Beneath the tree was a well, perhaps recalling the well of the giant Mímir? Every spring, a man was drowned there in sacrifice. Though firmly denounced by local churches, tree worship continued in Northern and Germanic Europe, as evidenced by maypole festivities and by the Christmas tree and winter solstice celebrations. ■

Odin's oracle

The runic "alphabet" is called the Futhark, after its first six letters (the "th" counts for a single letter). It appears to have been inspired by the Greek or Latin alphabet and was used from the early 1st century CE to the 9th century—though some people in rural Scandinavia could still read it at the end of the 20th century. Runes lack horizontal strokes because they were carved into wooden sticks, and horizontal strokes could be mistaken for wood grain and be less legible. The runes (which numbered 24, and later, 16) had a triple purpose. They were used to write short inscriptions, such as dedications, declarations of ownership, artisan signatures, spells, and hexes. Each rune also had a specific name and meaning; much like the Major Arcana in the Tarot of Marseille, they were used to predict the future. And finally, one could tap into runes' power by engraving or drawing them on an object or even one's skin. **D.D.L.T.**

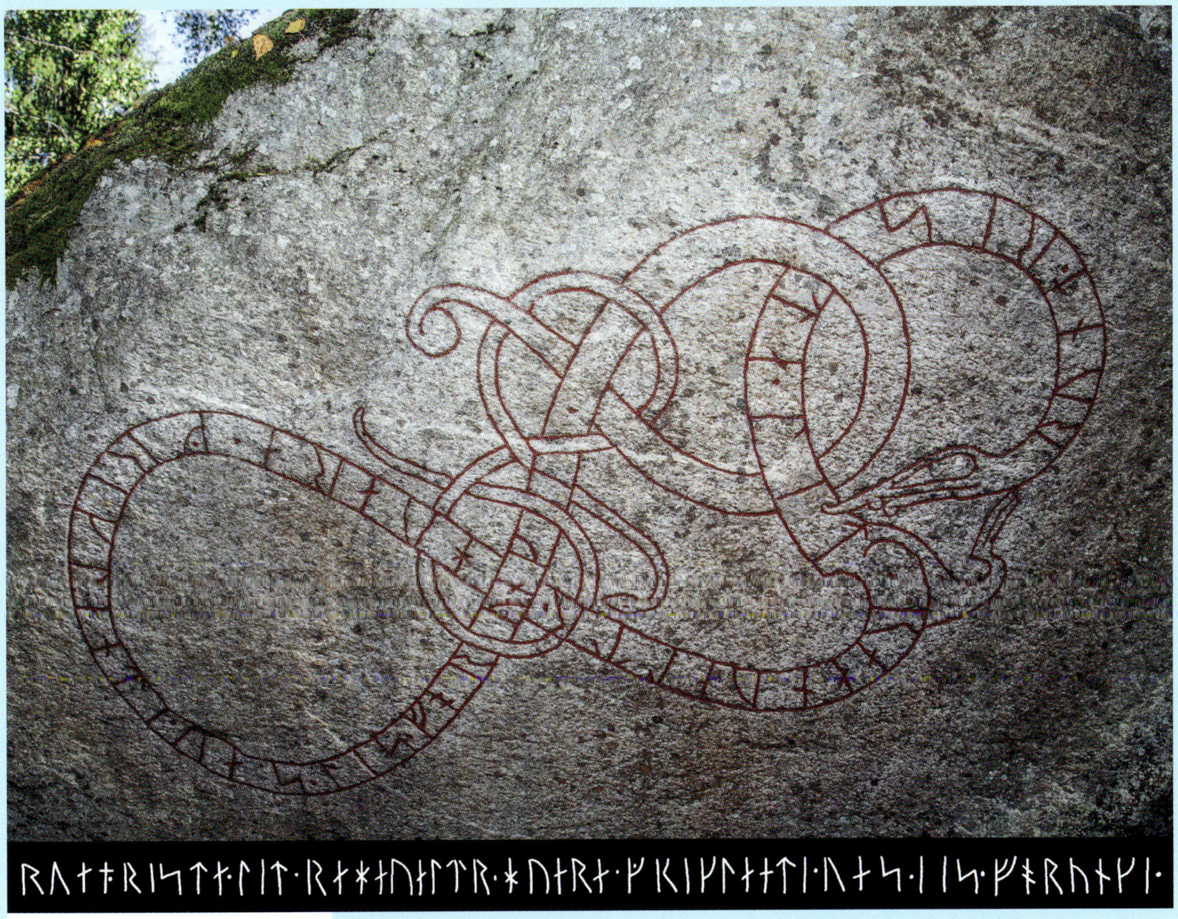

This runic inscription, found in Kyrkstigen, in the Swedish province of Uppland, north of Stockholm, was commissioned by a mercenary and former commander of the Byzantine emperor's Varangian Guard (Vikings from Russia). The text begins at the snake's head and continues along the animal's twisting body. Below it is a linear reproduction.

Phonetic transcription:
RUNA: RISTA: LIT: RAHNUALTR: HUAR: A: GRIKLANDI: UAS: LIS: FORUNKI:

Old Norse transcription:
Runar: rista: lét: Ragnvaldr: var: a: Grikklandi: vas: liths: forungi:

Literal translation:
Runes: engraved: were: Ragnvaldr: who: in: Greece: was: troop: commander:

Final translation
Ronald, who had these runes engraved, commanded the troops in Greece.

NB : Ragnvaldr, meaning "head of the council" or "who makes decisions" has morphed into various given names: Reginald, Reinhold, Roald, Ronald, Ronaldo, Renaud.

Gods and beasts

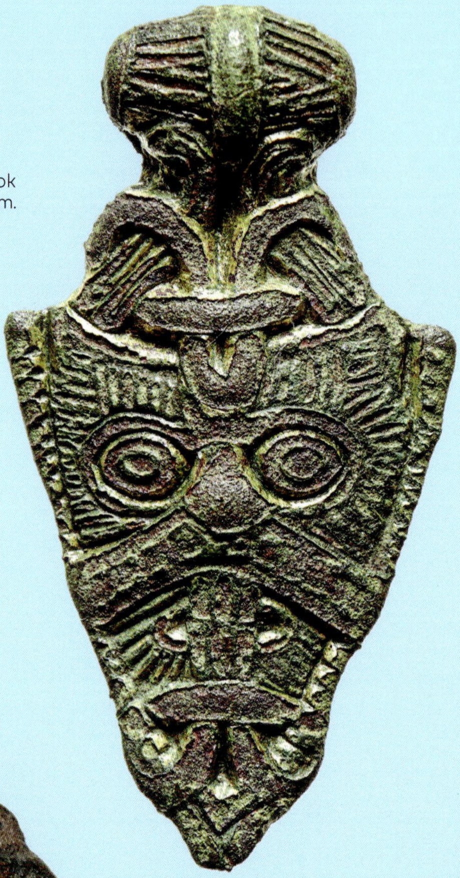

Pendant in the form of a mask

The Vikings were not bound to obey or worship their gods, but they performed rites such as sacrifices, held feasts, and took oaths to solidify their connection with them.

Bronze. Lille Lyngby.
National Museum of Denmark.

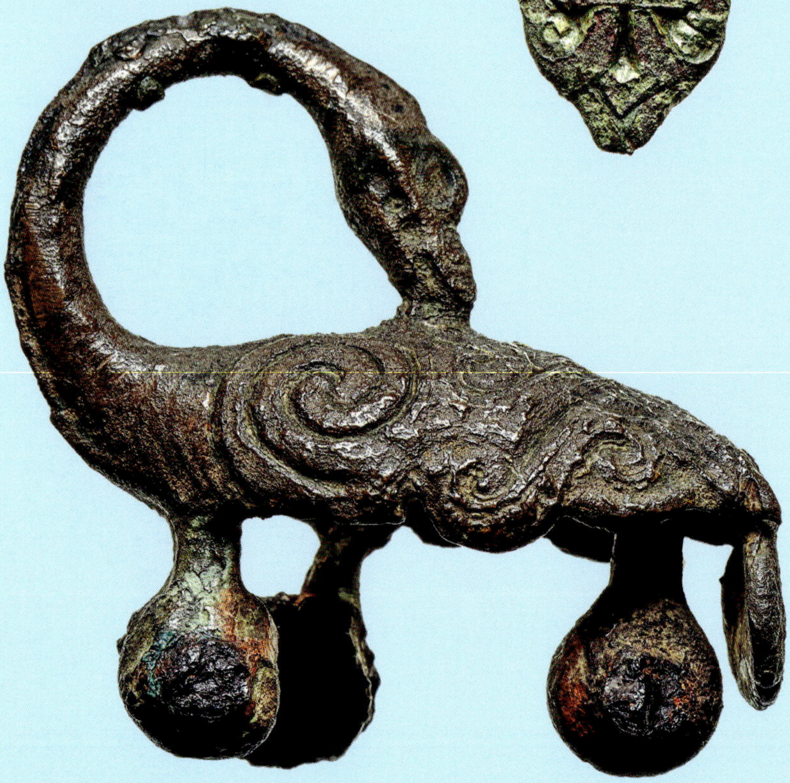

Swan-shaped terminals from a harness bow

In the *Prose Edda*, according to Viking mythology, two swans drink from the well of Urd. The water is so pure, everything that touches it turns white. This is how swans got their white plumage.

Bronze. Skellebæk.
900–1000 CE.
National Museum of Denmark.

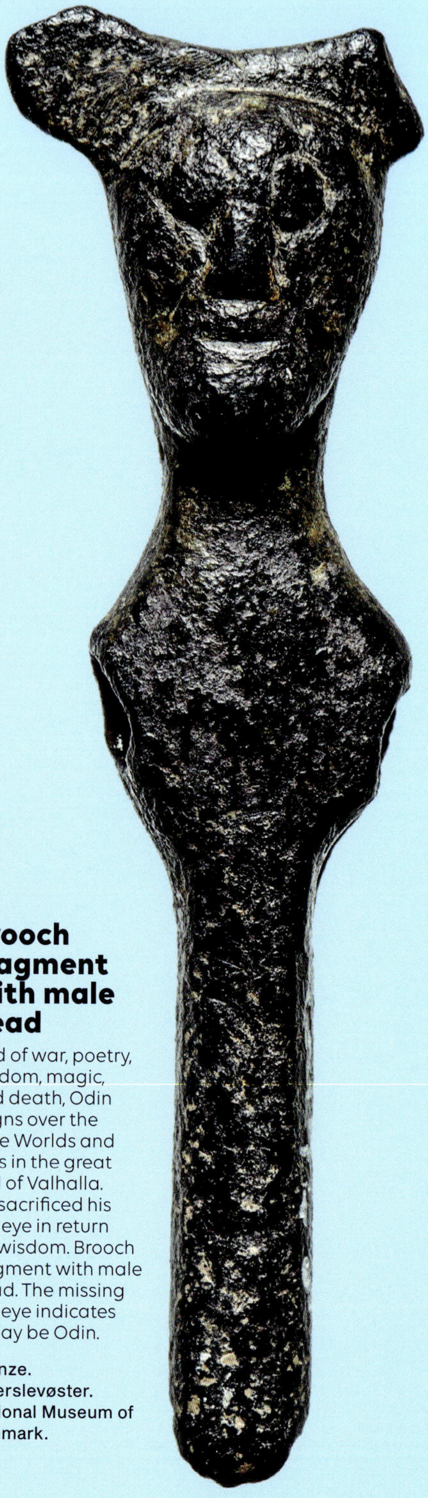

Brooch fragment with male head

God of war, poetry, wisdom, magic, and death, Odin reigns over the Nine Worlds and lives in the great hall of Valhalla. He sacrificed his left eye in return for wisdom. Brooch fragment with male head. The missing left eye indicates it may be Odin.

Bronze.
Sigerslevøster.
National Museum of Denmark.

Oval brooch, decorated with a twisted silver rod wire

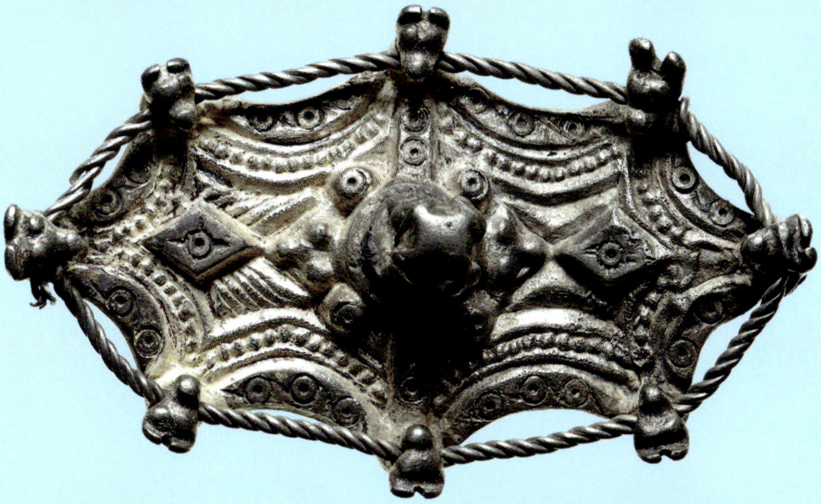

In the Viking universe, eight worlds perfectly counterbalanced each other, two by two. In the centre was Midgard, the ninth world, the world of humans. Vikings were meant to contribute to this balance by fulfilling their destiny with honour.

Silver. Oksenvad. 800–900 CE. National Museum of Denmark.

Pendant in shape of Mjolnir

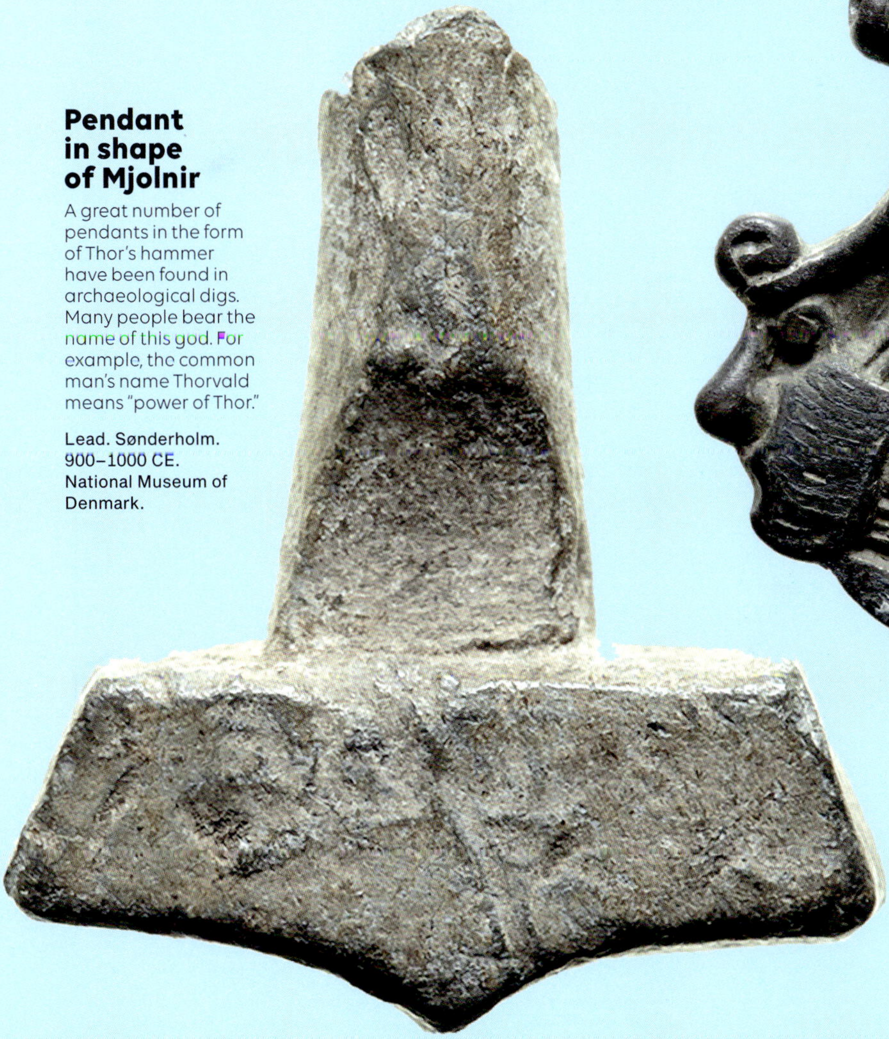

A great number of pendants in the form of Thor's hammer have been found in archaeological digs. Many people bear the name of this god. For example, the common man's name Thorvald means "power of Thor."

Lead. Sønderholm. 900–1000 CE. National Museum of Denmark.

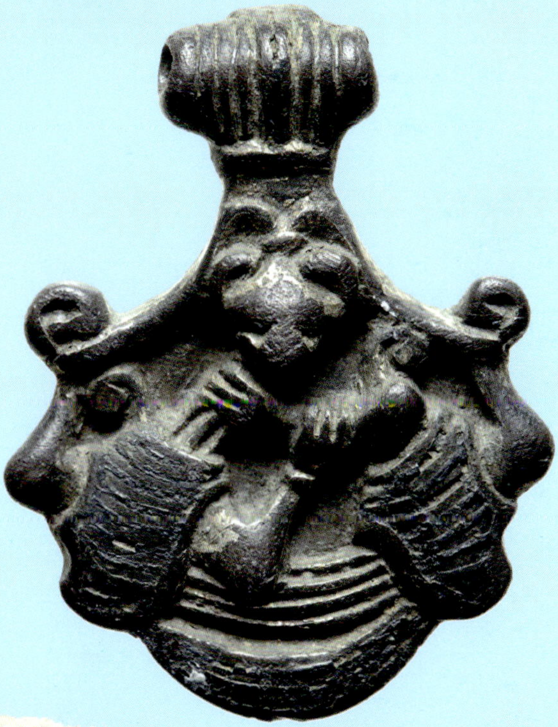

Pendant

Borre Style pendant decorated with a bear motif (linked with Odin) or cat motif (linked with Freyja). Viking art is highly influenced by nature and mythology. Many objects are elaborately decorated with depictions of animals such as birds or wolves.

Silver and gilt. Boeslunde. 800–975 CE. National Museum of Denmark.

EXPLORERS AND FAMOUS WARRIORS

Claude Pommereau

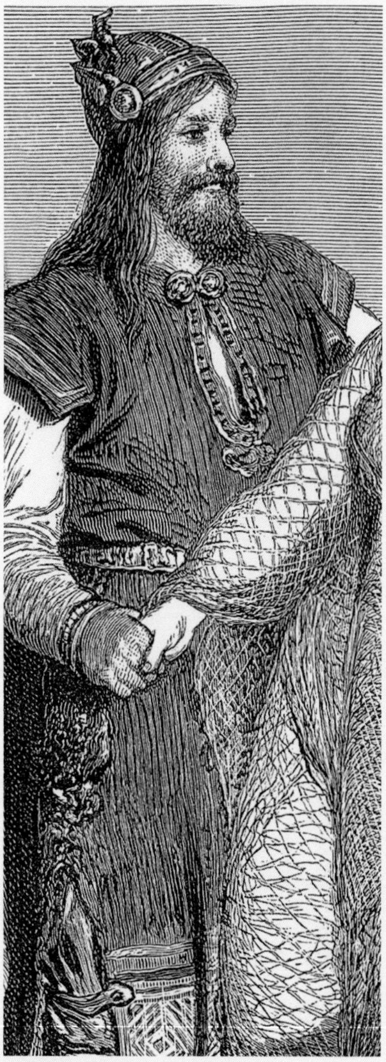

Ragnar Lodbrok
(circa 800–850)
Mythical warrior

A Viking chieftain during the famous attack on Paris of 845 and a semi-legendary figure (he is one of the heroes of the *Deeds of the Danes*, written circa 1200), he apparently tried to conquer England with two ships! It is said that he was imprisoned by the King of Northumberland and died when he was thrown into a pit of venomous snakes. Many of the feats attributed to him may well be the deeds of other Viking heroes.

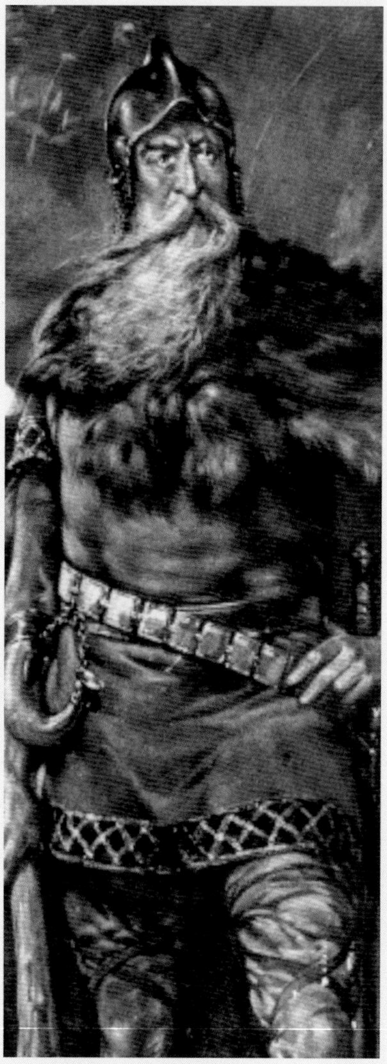

Rurik (or Ryorik) (830–879)
The Rus'

This chieftain, who founded the rich principality of Novgorod, was a Varangian and a member of Swedish trading expeditions to the east. His son Oleg extended his trade routes to Kyiv, conquering a vast territory and founding a dynasty. His state was later swept away by the Mongols in 1240. It is seldom acknowledged in Russia that the first "Rus" state emerged under Varangian leadership.

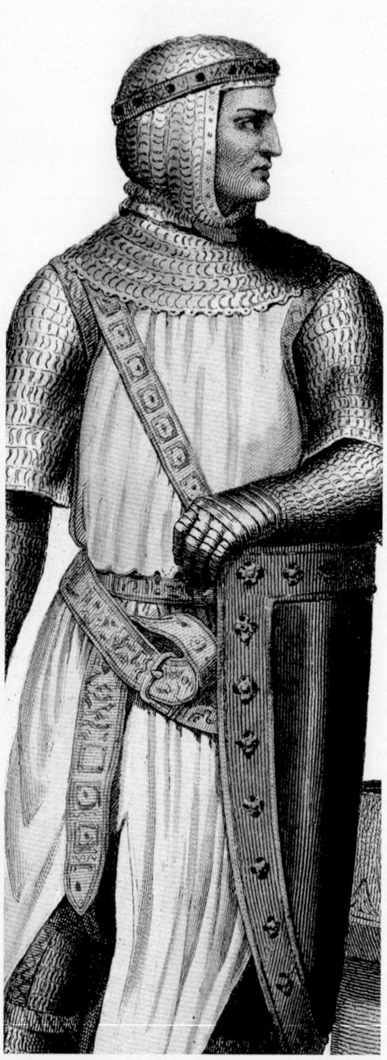

Rollo (circa 846–932)
Founder of Normandy

Where did this Jarl, or Viking chieftain, come from? Perhaps from Norway. Accompanied by a band of mostly Danish warriors, he set up camp at the mouth of the Seine to conduct raids. In 911, at Saint-Clair-sur-Epte the Frankish king Charles the simple, weary of his raids and plundering, granted him sovereignty over "the region between the Andelle and the sea" on the condition that he convert to Christianity and put an end to his raids.

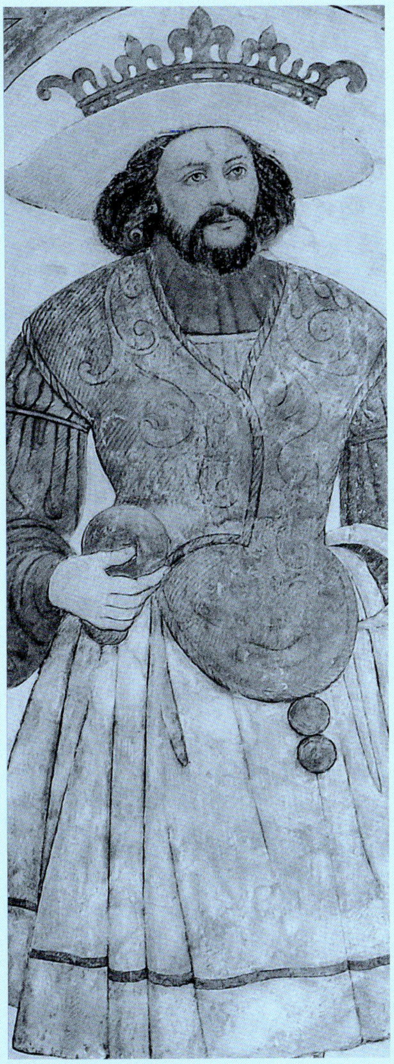

Harald Bluetooth
(circa 910–983)
Converter of Denmark

King of Denmark and Norway, he claimed to have Christianized the Danes. The runic inscription on the large Jelling Stone in Jutland pays tribute to his parents and proclaims Christianity as the official religion of Denmark. The stone confirms his role in the revolution in morals and beliefs of many Scandinavian populations.

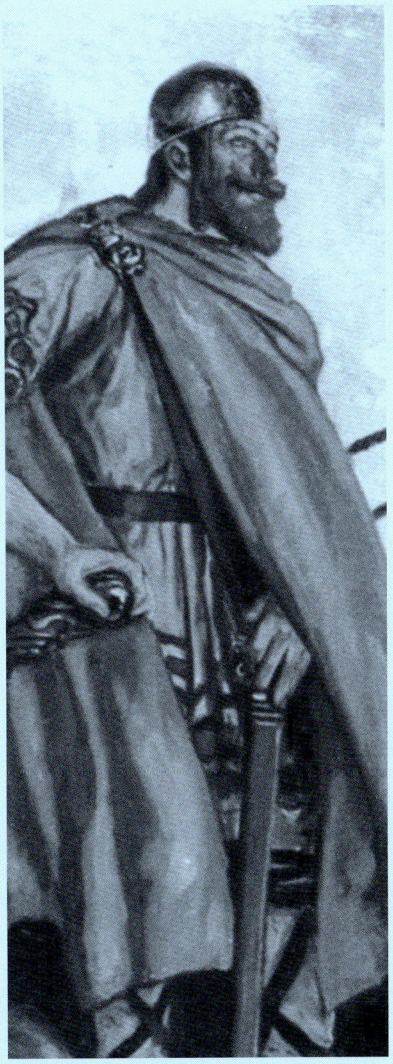

Erik the Red (940–circa 1010)
Settler of Greenland

Eirikr Thorvaldson bore the epithet "the Red" because of his red hair and beard. Accused of murder, he left Iceland in 962 and discovered Greenland. He settled the fertile coast of the island four years later, along with 1,000 Icelandic colonists, for whom he would become a respected chieftain. His son Leifr would later go on to discover Vinland.

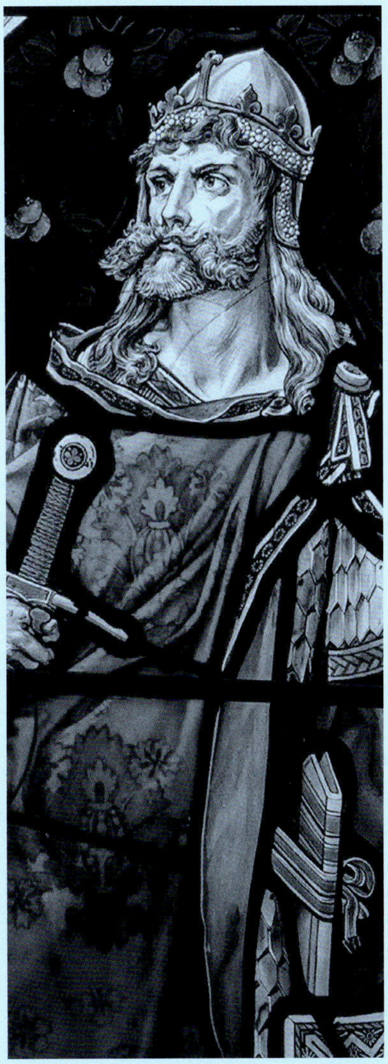

Harald Hardrada (1015–1066)
"The Stern"

King of Norway from 1046 until his death. After losing battles against the English king, he travelled to Kyiv and then Constantinople, where he joined the Byzantine emperor's Varangian Guard. After fighting for the emperor all over the world, he returned to Norway, where King Magnus had made him his heir. He later contested for the crown of England and was killed in the Battle of Stamford Bridge.

The above images are 19th-century illustrations.

Saga of the Journey

"From there, they sailed with a north-easterly wind and were two days and nights at sea before seeing land, toward which they sailed, arriving at an island which lay northward of the mainland. Deciding to prepare to spend the winter there, they built a large house. There was plentiful salmon in the river and lake, and larger than any they had seen before. The land was so good that they thought the livestock would have no need of fodder in winter, for there was no frost in winter, and the grass barely withered there."

Excerpt from the *Saga of the Greenlanders*, chapter 3

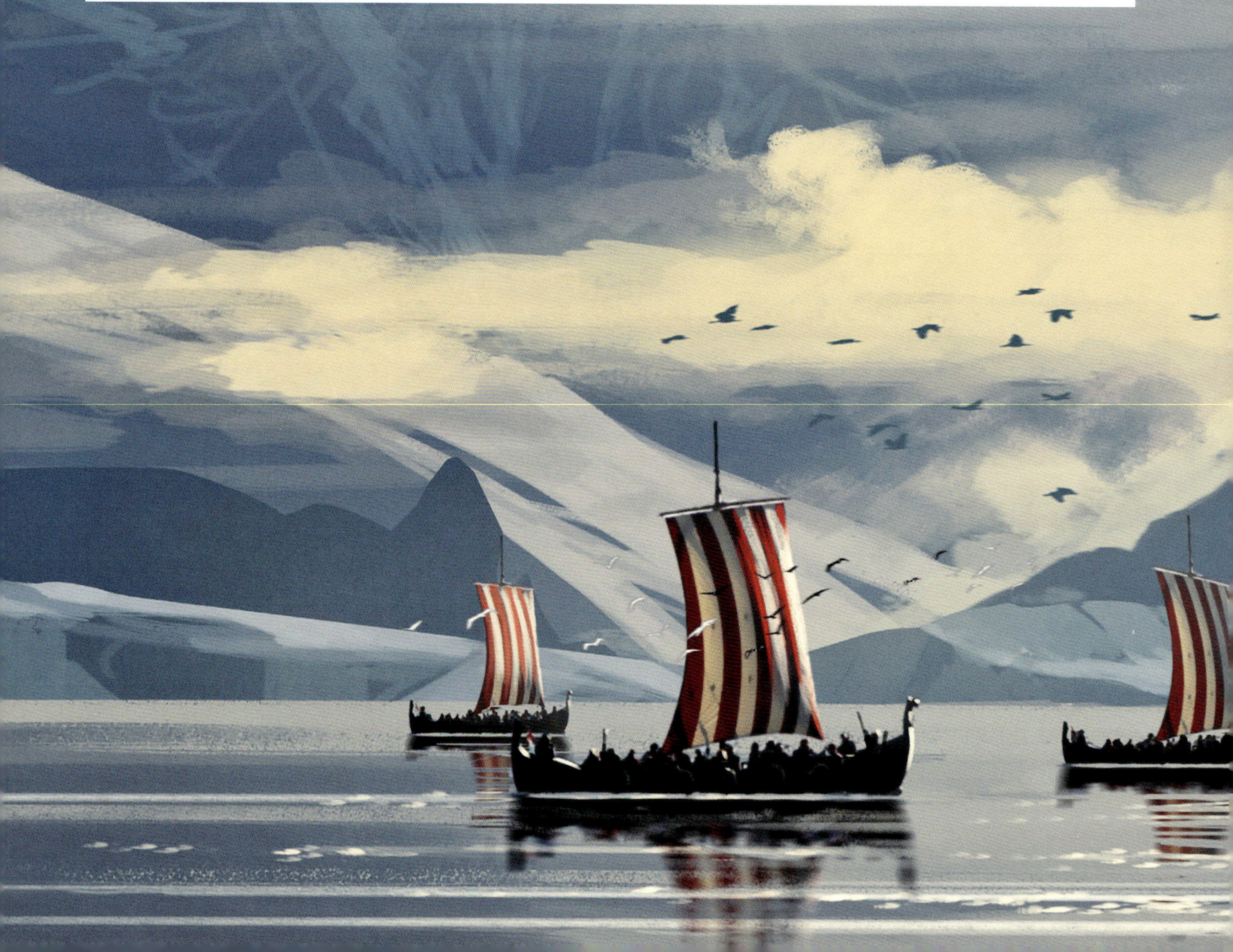

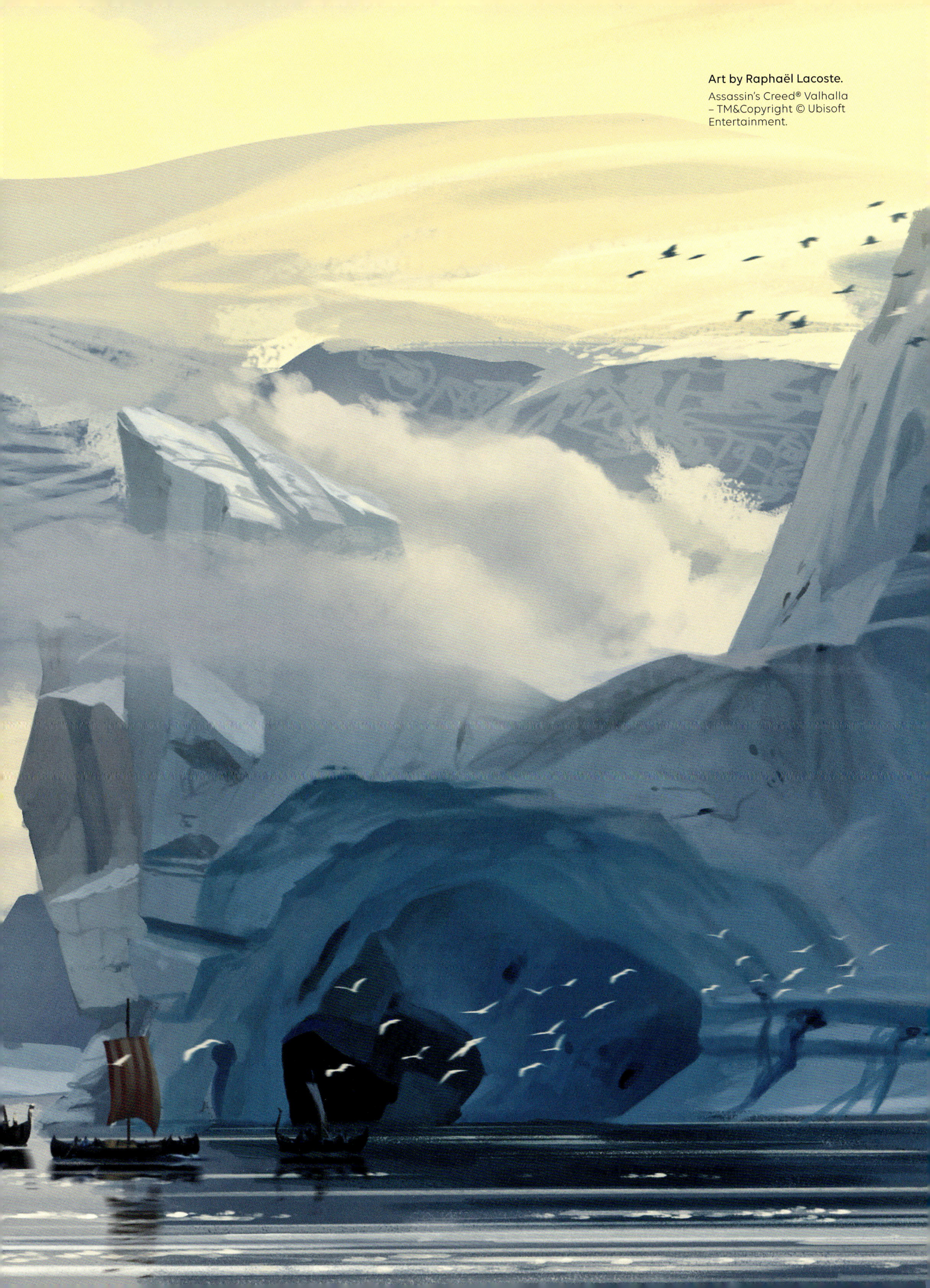

Art by Raphaël Lacoste.

Exploring the world

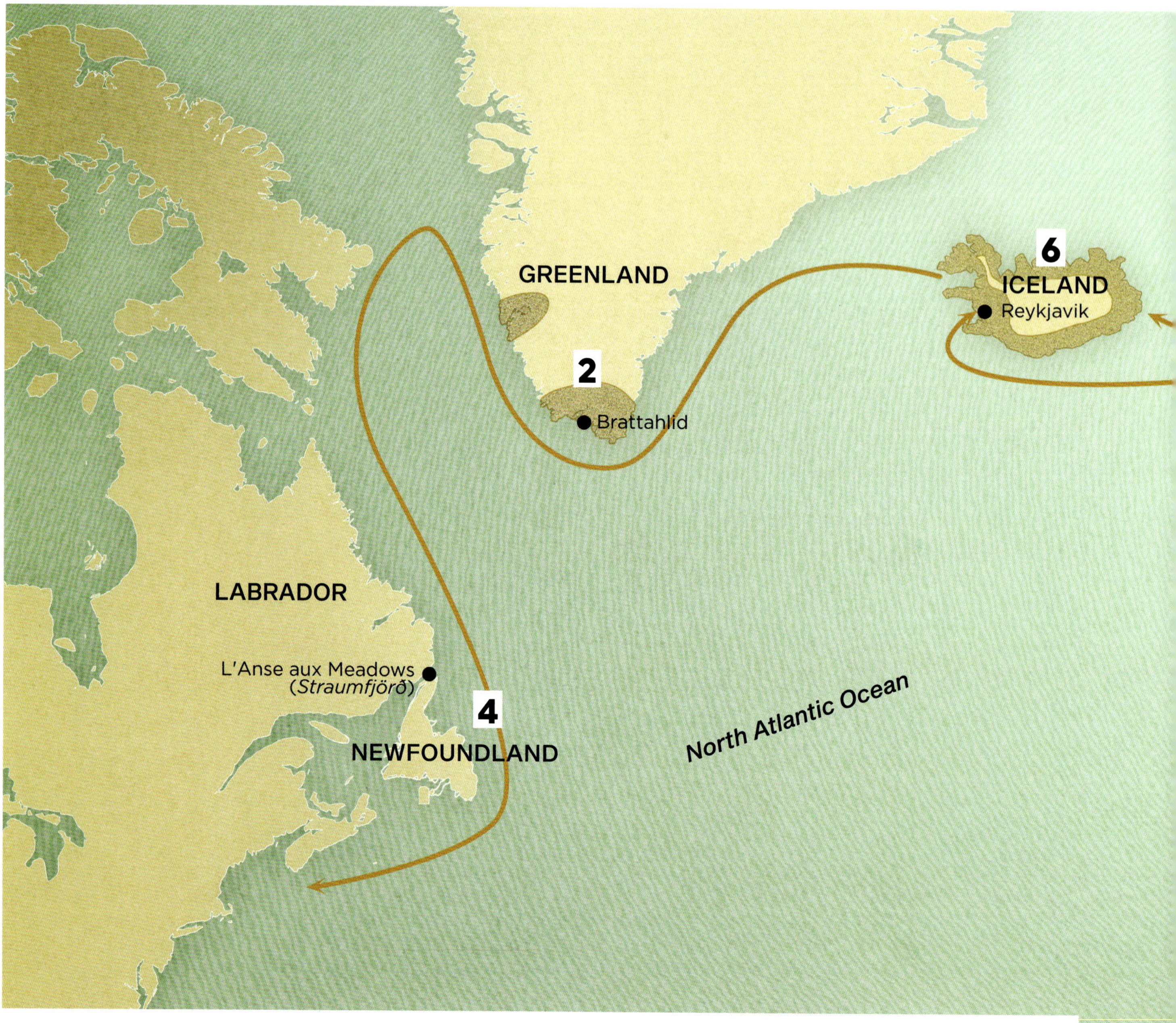

1. Staraïa Ladoga
The main trading outpost of the "Rus'" Varangians in the 8th and 9th centuries, located on the road to Novgorod. Ladoga was the name of the river and the lake. Might it have been the first capital of "Russia"?

2. Brattahlid
The name of Erik the Red's estate in Greenland. Located on a fjord that sheltered it from storms. His descendants lived there until the 15th century.

3. Dorestad
An important port in its heyday of the 9th century. Located on an arm of the Rhine delta, the Vikings flourished there from 850 to 885.

4. Vinland
Icelandic adventurer Leif Erikson explored the east coast of North America. The Vikings settled in L'Anse aux Meadows, Newfoundland, in 1021.

5. Paris
Besieged several times by the Vikings, including in 845. In 911, the Treaty of Saint-Clair-sur-Epte, allowed the Vikings to settle in Normandy on the condition that they protect the realm from other Viking incursions.

6. Iceland
The first Viking settlements in Iceland were established in 873 by Norwegians fleeing attempts by Harald Fairhair to create a Norwegian kingdom.

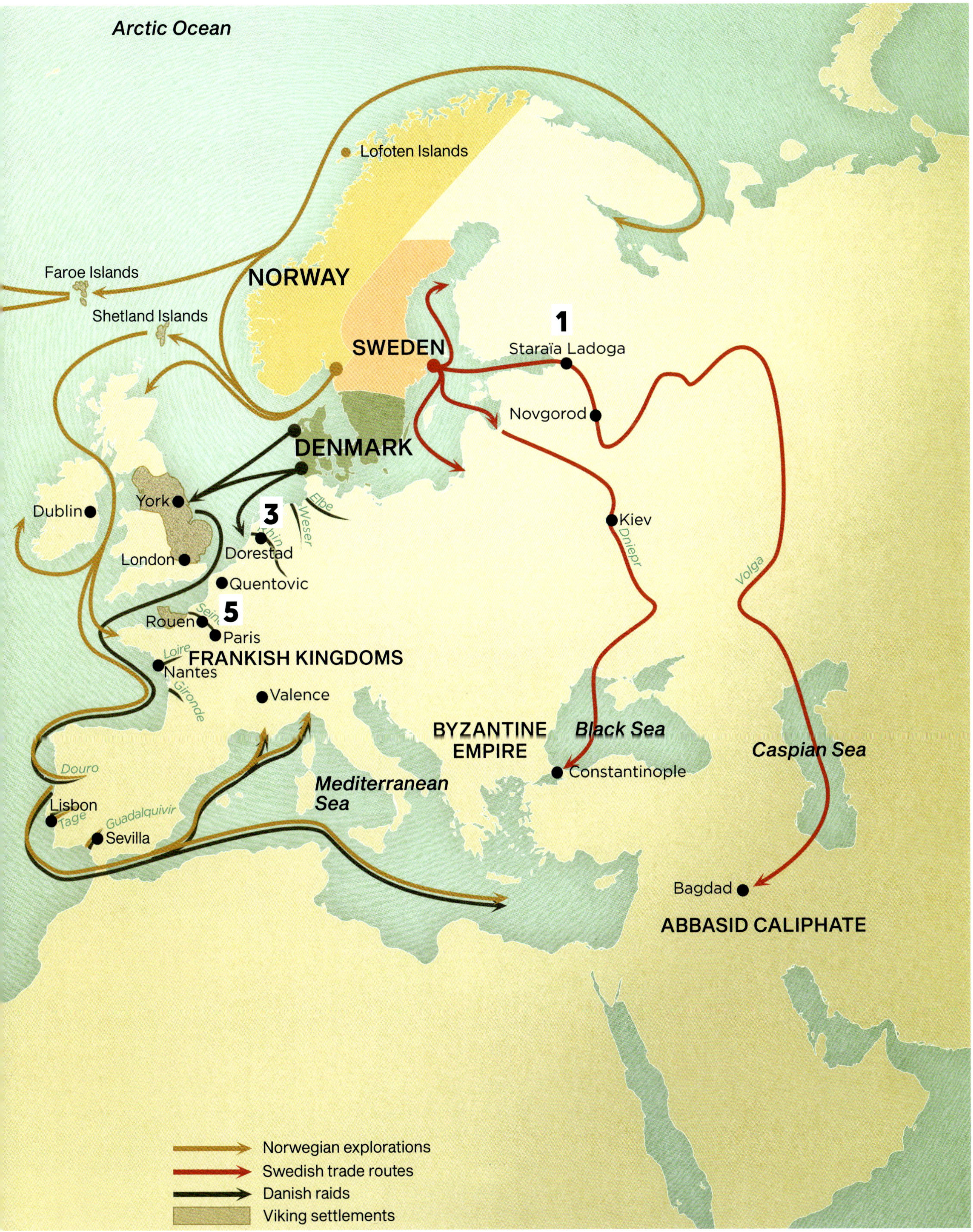
Arctic Ocean
Lofoten Islands
Faroe Islands
NORWAY
Shetland Islands
1
SWEDEN
Staraïa Ladoga
Novgorod
DENMARK
York
Dublin
3
Elbe
Weser
Kiev
Dniepr
Dorestad
London
Quentovic
Volga
5
Rouen
Seine
Paris
Loire
FRANKISH KINGDOMS
Nantes
Gironde
Valence
BYZANTINE EMPIRE
Black Sea
Caspian Sea
Douro
Constantinople
Mediterranean Sea
Lisbon
Tage
Guadalquivir
Sevilla
Bagdad
ABBASID CALIPHATE
Norwegian explorations
Swedish trade routes
Danish raids
Viking settlements

Lightweight, sturdy ships

THE SAIL MADE THE WORLD SMALLER

Peter Pentz, curator at the National Museum of Denmark

The knowledge and skills that Vikings used to build ships had been gathered and refined over many centuries. The Norse had been a sailing people for a long time. Shipbuilders in the Viking Age were skilled craftsmen and their tools were highly specialized. Tasks all the way down to choosing materials required special competence. Clever shipwrights who knew about the nature and structure of trees and wood carefully selected their timbers. Some parts of the ships required wood that had grown in a particular way. By exploiting the diversity of nature, shipbuilders could create light, but still extremely strong vessels. This proved crucial when the ships put out to sea. Some runestones tell about shipwrecks and drownings. The development of the ultimate Viking ship cost many human lives.

The ships, as a rule, were rowboats, but in the years leading up to the Viking Age, ships were equipped with a mast and a sail, allowing them to travel more quickly and over greater distances. For the Vikings, who measured distance in time, this meant that the world became smaller. In less than a day, a warship from Zealand, Denmark, could cross the Baltic Sea and reach North Germany.

From east to west, from north to south

The world of the Vikings stretched from the Black Sea and the Caspian Sea, in the east, to North America, in the west. From Lofoten Islands in Norway, in the north, to the Mediterranean and North Africa, in the south. Throughout Central Europe and the Middle East, one could obtain products from Asia, China and the area around the Indian Ocean. We do not know for sure how far the Vikings journeyed into Asia. An Arabian source from the 800s claims that the Vikings reached China and traded there.

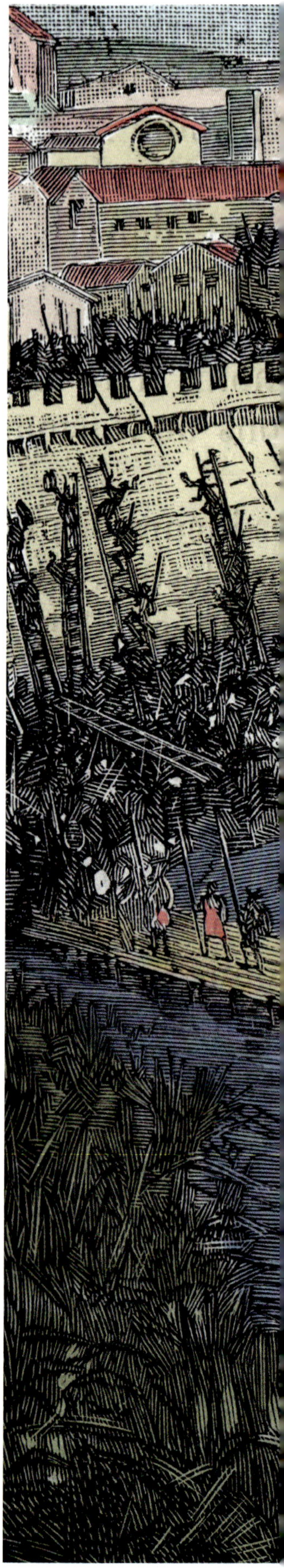

RIGHT

Led by Rollo, the Normans lay seige to Paris in 885.
1884. Colour lithography.

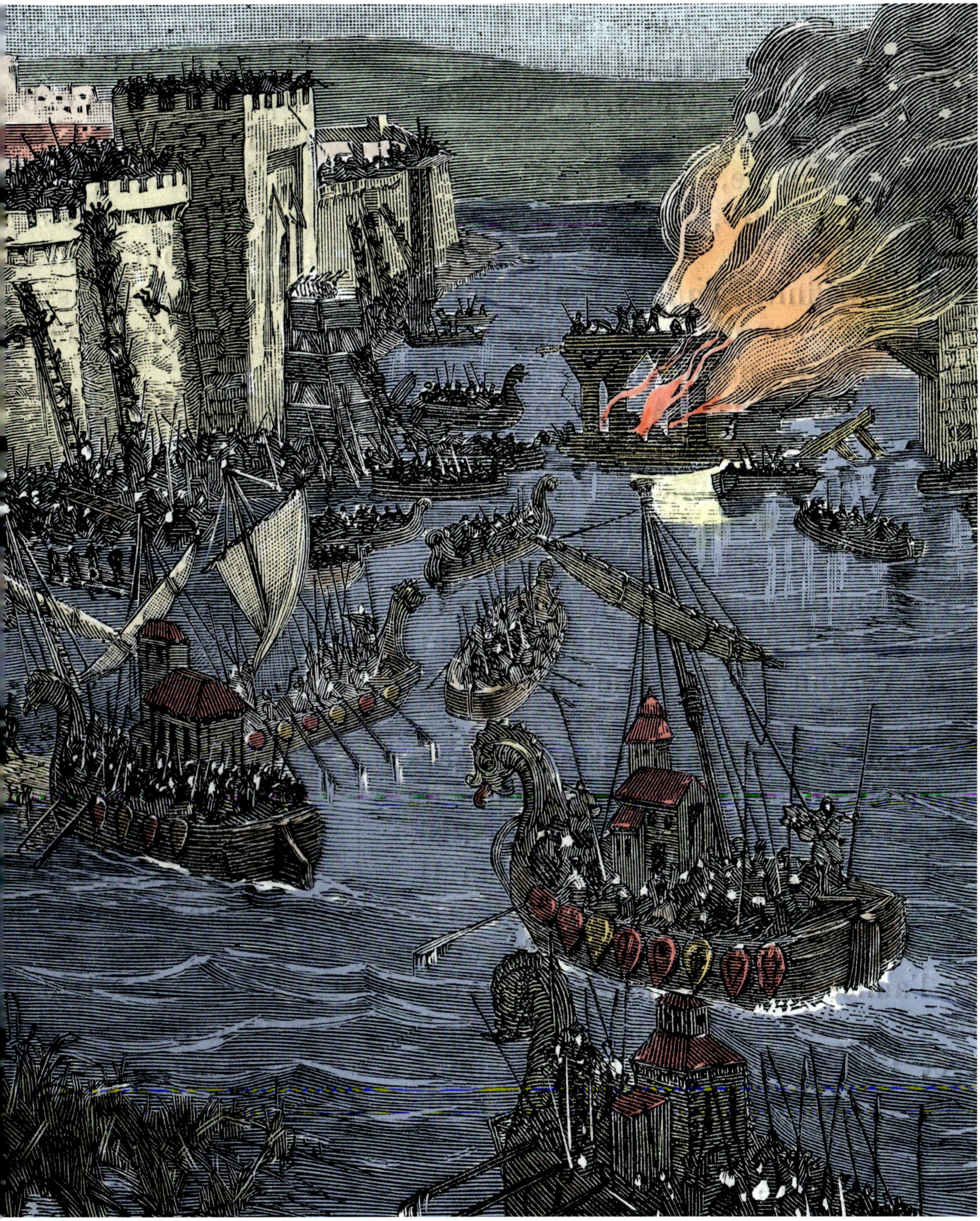

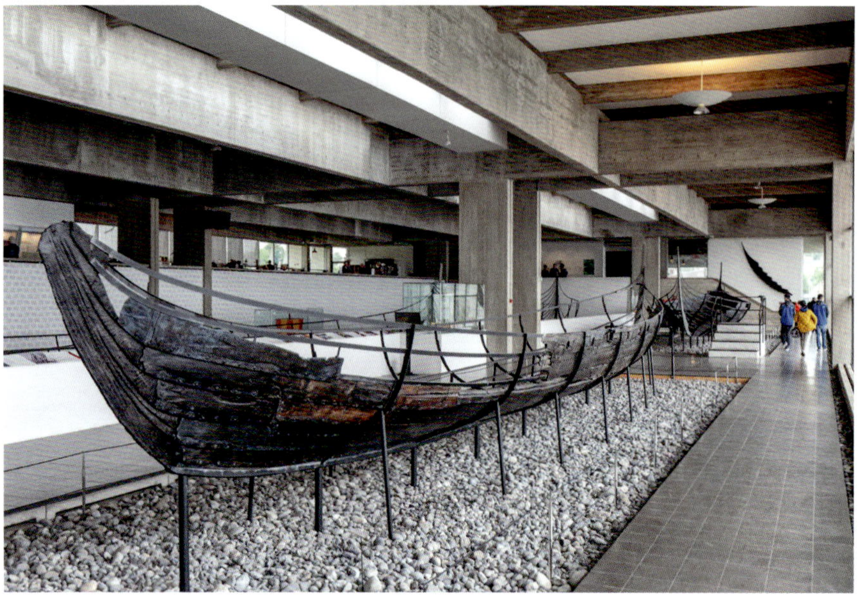

ABOVE
Ship's hull at the Viking Ship Museum in Roskilde, Denmark.

Greed, a spirit of adventure and the pursuit of fame were certainly motives for the Vikings' journeys. But following in the wake of the Viking ships was an increase in the interaction between nations. The flow of articles, products, people and capital ran faster than ever before. Ideas and culture were exchanged with a new haste. The culture of the Vikings became a mixed culture created by encounters with others. A Buddha from Afghanistan was buried in a Viking grave in Central Sweden and a returned Icelander proudly showed off his impressive Byzantine robes among the residents of the island. No society, farm or family was unaffected. No one could stand alone, be self-contained or independent. The world had become a more interconnected place.

Raiding, conquering and settlement

When the first Viking ships set sail to go on plundering raids, they were just continuing and developing a practice that had existed for centuries. Plundering was not only regarded as an activity which provided goods and gold. The honour attained through thieving was considered almost more important than riches and the Viking leaders and king were obligated to share their new wealth amongst the warriors, noblemen and peasants. The kings who did not do this were not kings for long.

One of the sagas tells of a man who travelled as a merchant for one half of the year and was on raids—"I Viking"—for the other half. For some people, the raids were seasonal work, these people were a kind of part-time Viking.

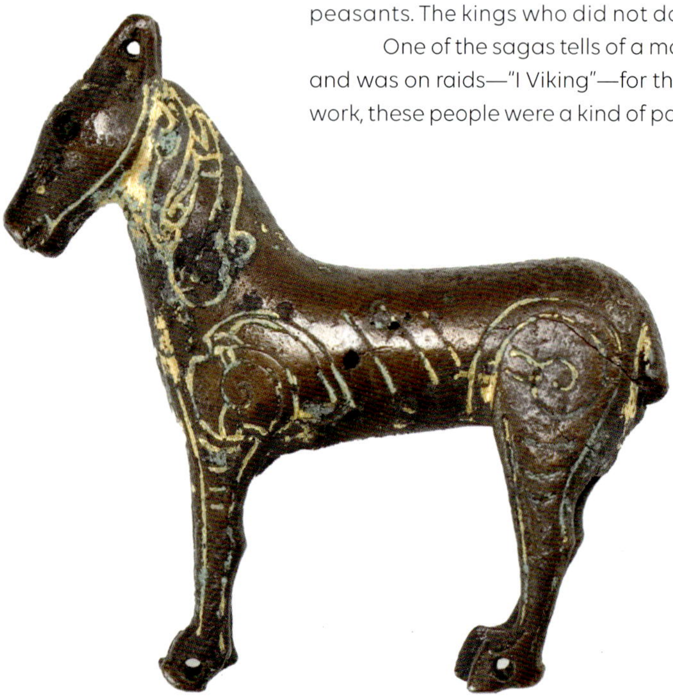

Weathervane's decoration

Weathervanes mounted at the top of the mast or bow indicated wind direction while adding a decorative touch to the vessel. This little horse would have been attached to an elaborate weathervane.

Gilt copper alloy. Lolland.
1000–1050 CE.
National Museum of Denmark.

Important dates in the Viking Age

793
Viking raid on the Lindisfarne Priory. This event is regarded as the beginning of the Viking Age. Early Viking raids targeted weakly defended coastal communities.

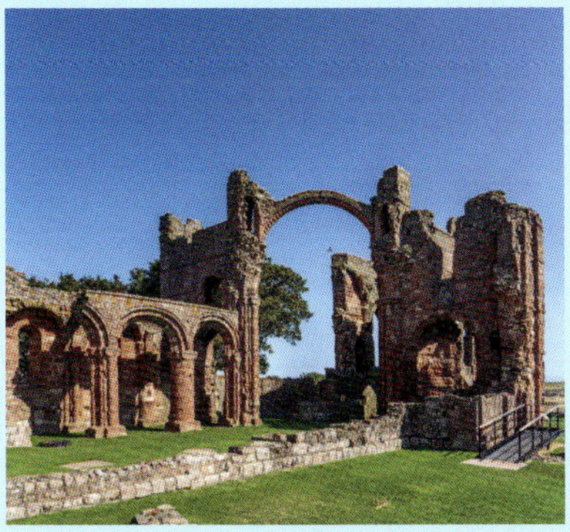

Late 8th century
The Vikings establish trading posts at Staraja Ladoga and Novgorod. Vikings known as the Rus' and Varangian peoples create principalities from the Baltic to the North Sea.

845
Siege of Paris.

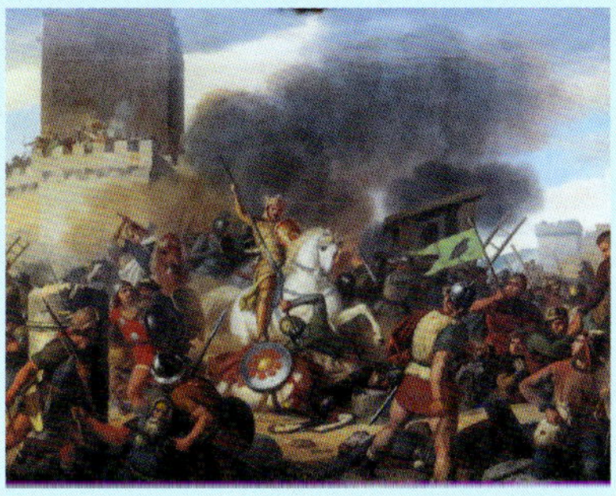

851
Viking attack on London. Norse people settle in Dublin and York, some of them permanently.

Circa 873–874
First Viking settlement in Iceland by Norwegians fleeing attempts by Harald Fairhair to make Norway a monarchy.

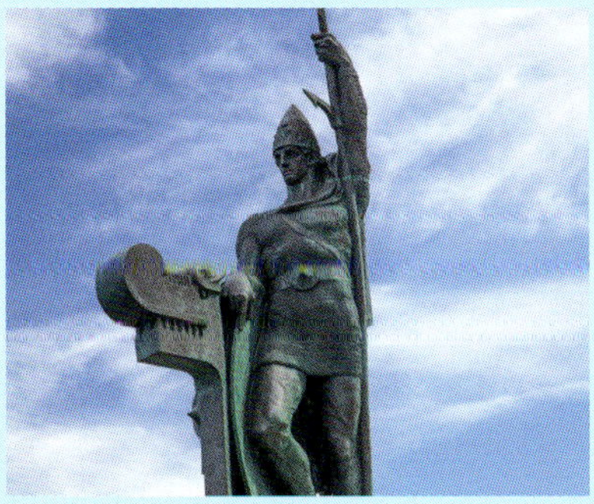

878
Alfred the Great, king of Wessex, defeats the Vikings at Eddington in southwest England. The Danes convert to Christianity and retreat to their own English territory, under the "Danelaw."

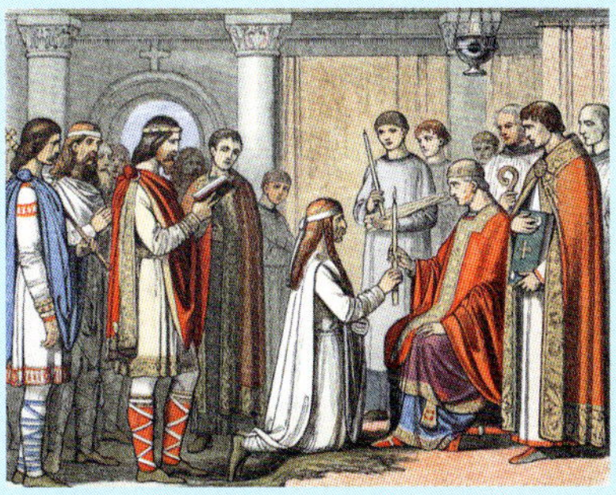

911
The king of the Franks and the Viking chieftain Rollo sign the Treaty of Saint-Clair-sur-Epte, which allows the Vikings to establish colonies in Normandy in exchange for protecting the kingdom against other Viking invasions.

Circa 960
Harald Bluetooth, king of Denmark, converts to Christianity. It marks the beginning of gradual transition to Christianity.

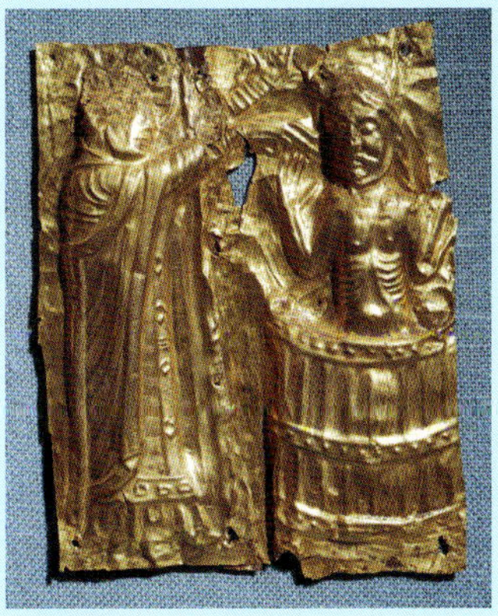

985
Led by Erik the Red, the Vikings settle Greenland.

Circa 990
The Byzantine emperor creates a Viking mercenary unit: the Varangian Guard.

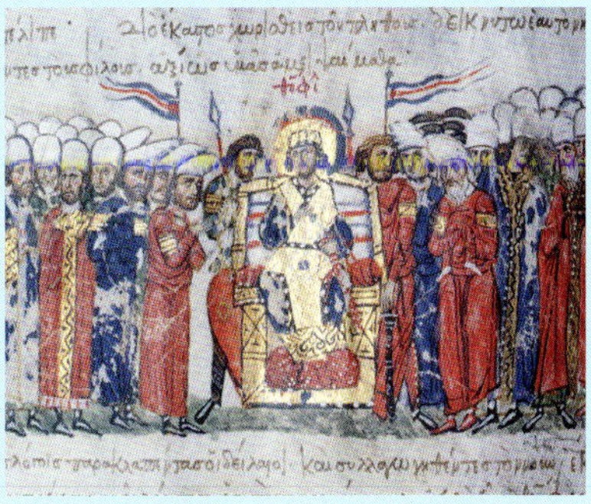

995
Olaf Tryggvason, king of Norway, unifies the chiefdoms under one kingdom. His attempt to force Christianity on the country causes the Norwegian nobility to revolt.

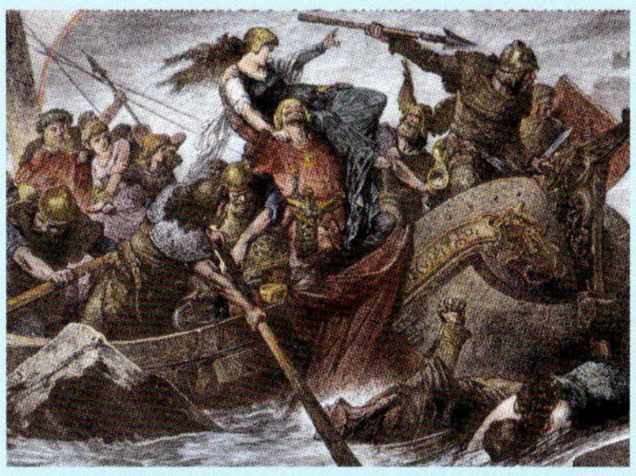

Circa 1000
Icelandic explorer Leif Erikson journeys to the east coast of North America.

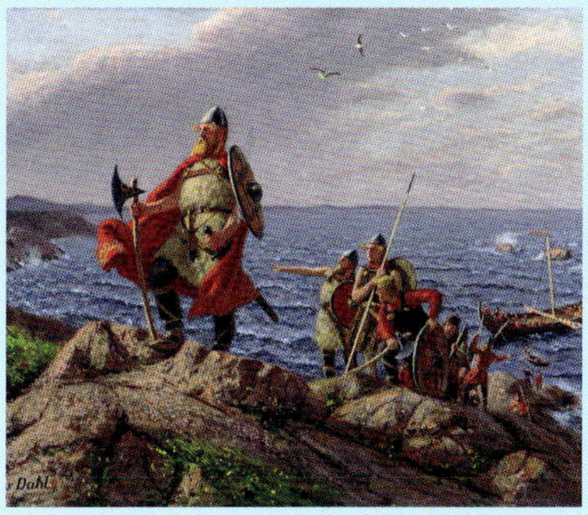

1021
Vikings establish a settlement at L'Anse aux Meadows, Newfoundland

September 1066
Harald Hardrada, king of Norway, tries to invade England but is killed at the Battle of Stamford Bridge.

October 1066
Led by William the Conqueror, the Normans defeat the Anglo-Saxons at Hastings. This battle, and the Battle of Stamford Bridge are generally seen as marking the end of the Viking Age.

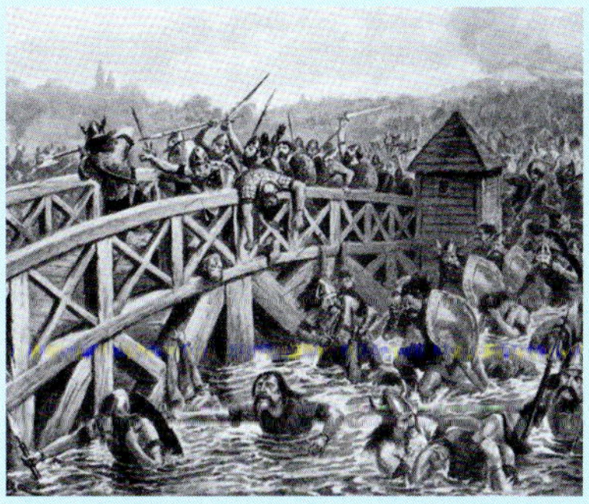

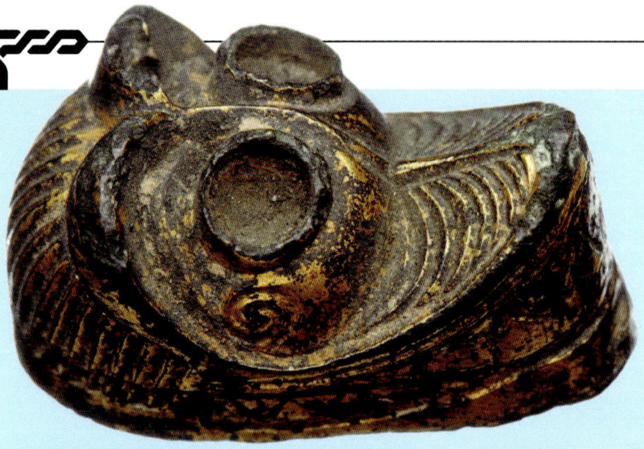

Scale weight in the form of an animal head

In the absence of a common currency, pieces of silver and fragments of jewelry were exchanged for goods. The weight of the precious metal determined its value.

Gilded silver.
National Museum of Denmark.

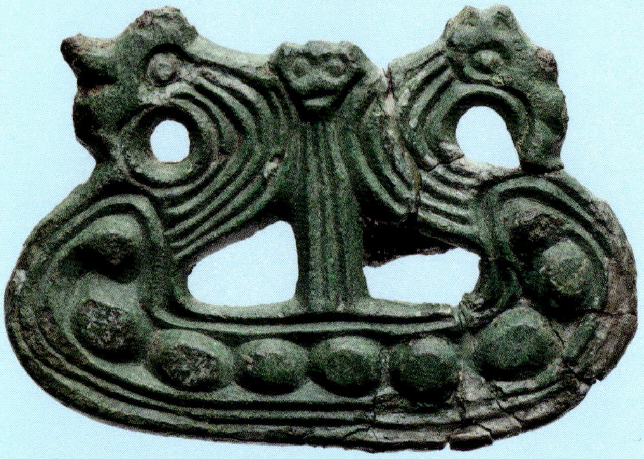

Brooch shaped like a ship

This horse-boat motif was very common in the Viking world and was associated with the god Freyr. He has a magical boat that folds up and fits in a pocket.

Bronze. Bornholm. 775–900 CE.
National Museum of Denmark.

By the middle of the 9th century, the extent of the Vikings' plundering and conquering seems to have grown. Huge fleets now set out from the fjords and inlets, not just from Scandinavia, but also from conquered regions and new towns, for example, Dublin. The fleets could contain hundreds of ships, under the leadership of a king, earl or chieftain.

They had a system called "leding," in which the free peasants were required to provide ships, crew and provision; first and foremost, to defend the country, but also when the king decided to go on large plundering raids.

At the same time as the plundering raids, which only had the aim of bringing goods and the gold back to their homelands, many people headed out to find a new life, far away from Scandinavia.

From around 875 and through the 900s, the Vikings populated the Faroe Islands and Iceland. This was part of an expansion, where (especially Norwegian) Viking settled in Scotland and surrounding islands.

The settlers had various reasons for wishing to leave their homeland. Some were simply unwanted, others were trying their luck. Some were chieftains, who had fallen out with their king and were taking a chance at continuing their life of prosperity somewhere else. But there were also women who went to Iceland on their own initiative, like the widow Audr, who was among the first settlers. In Iceland, the Vikings created a society without a king but a common council, a "thing." The colonisation of Iceland was part of the Viking expansions to the west, which also came to include settlement in the fjords along the west coast of Greenland and, for a short time, the north coast of Newfoundland in Canada.

As early as the start of the Viking Age, Danish chieftains had settled in the Frankish areas in Friesland, after disputes and negotiations with the Franks.

To the west, the Vikings overwintered in Ireland for the first time in 841—instead of just raiding and sailing home again. They founded the city of Dublin with a Viking king residing in his own little kingdom. Far to the east, in Russia and Ukraine, Swedish and other Vikings living around the Baltic Sea settled in Russia in the 800s.

During the 870s, the Viking settled in eastern England, this was the start of a long conquest which ended with Danish hegemony by the end of the Viking Age. Some of the Vikings who had participated in battles in England continued to Normandy, where in 911, the Frankish king handed over vast areas of land to the Viking chieftain Rollo.

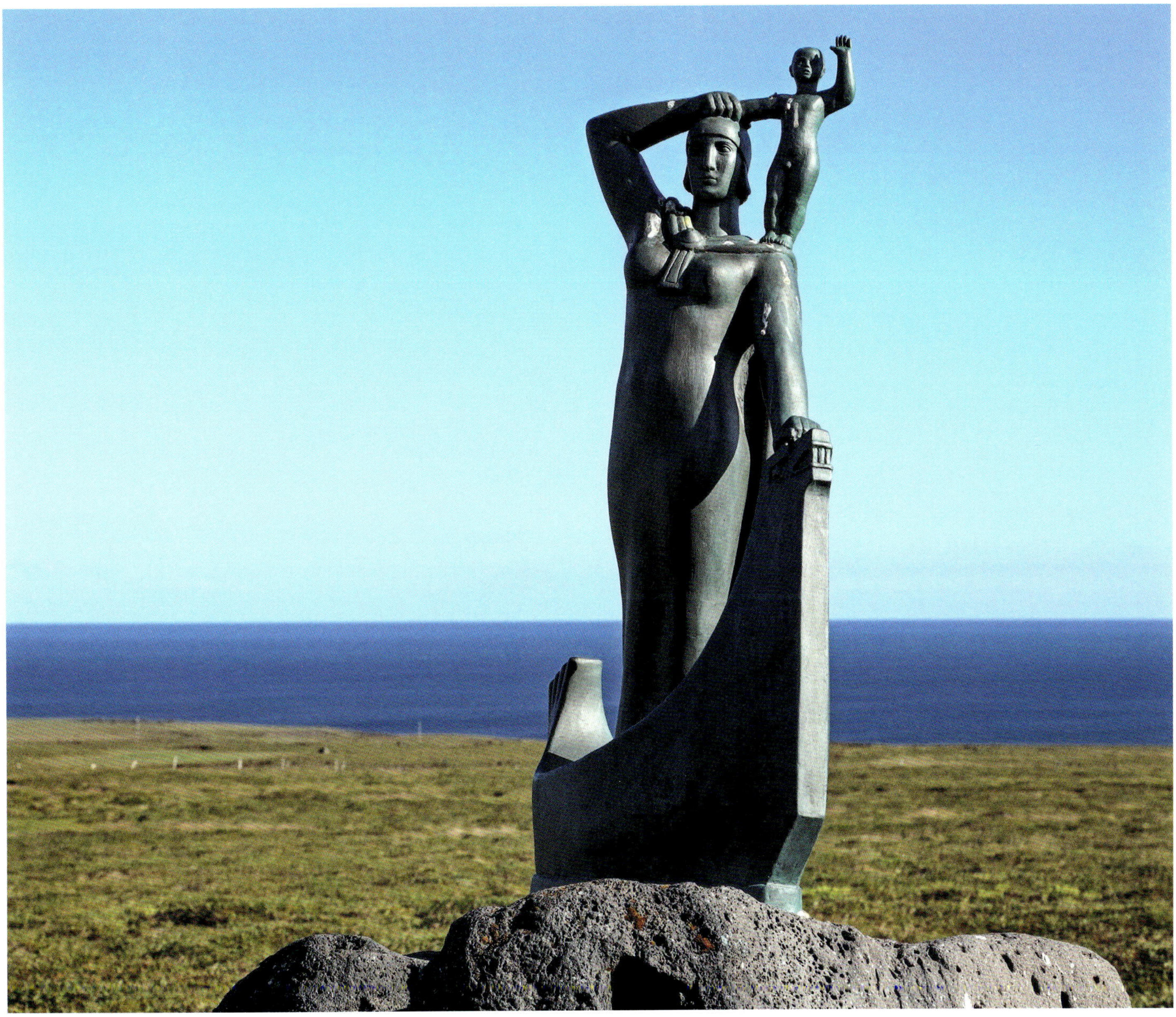

The Vikings' plundering and ravaging was a great plague, especially for Europe, in the three centuries. But many of the battles the Vikings fought took place at home in Scandinavia. Warlords, kings and petty kings fought against each other, not so much because they wanted to acquire gold and silver, but more to achieve command over as many areas as possible. It was from these disputes that the three kingdoms of Norway, Sweden and Denmark emerged out of the Viking Age.

Plundering, fighting and destruction left Europe wounded, while the aggressive Viking nations developed into European kingdoms. But as the wounds turned into scars—visible reminders of a turbulent and violent era—the impact of Viking settlements were more permanent. In the areas that were already populated, language, place names, lifestyle and rules blended together with the culture of the native inhabitants. This can be traced today, especially In the British Isles, northern France and, to some extent, in Russia. Common English words such as "call" and "die" have their Scandinavian roots in "kalde" and "do." In Normandy, you can visit the town of Holbec, which is also the name of the town of Zealand in Denmark—Holbaek. In Russia you might meet a girl called Olga, which comes from the Norse name Helga. ■

ABOVE
Gudrid Thorbjarnardóttir was among the first European women to settle in the Americas. She was the mother of Snorri, the first European born in North America. After converting to Christianity, she made a pilgrimage to Rome and, upon returning to Iceland, became a nun.

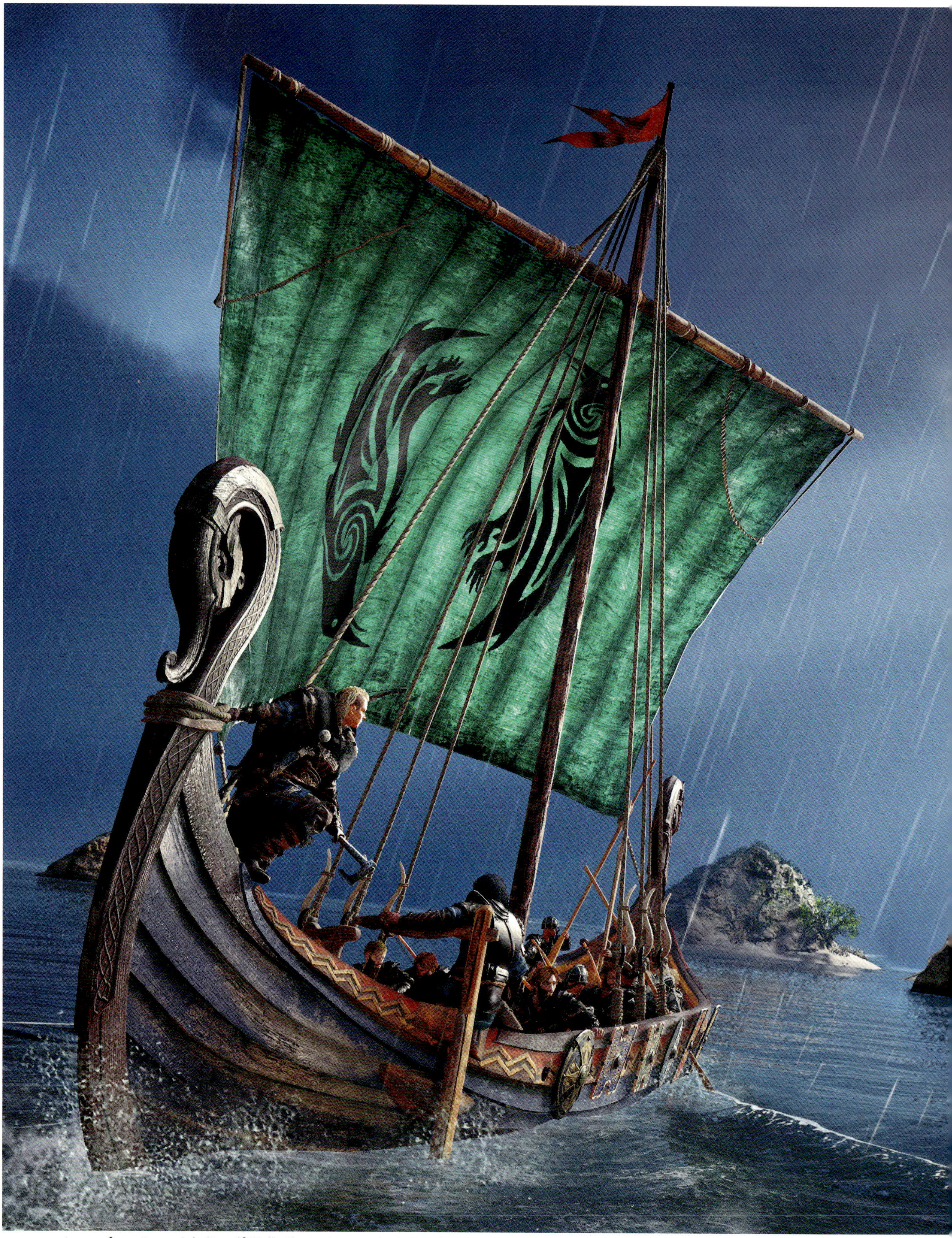

Image from Assassin's Creed® Valhalla. TM&Copyright © Ubisoft Entertainment.

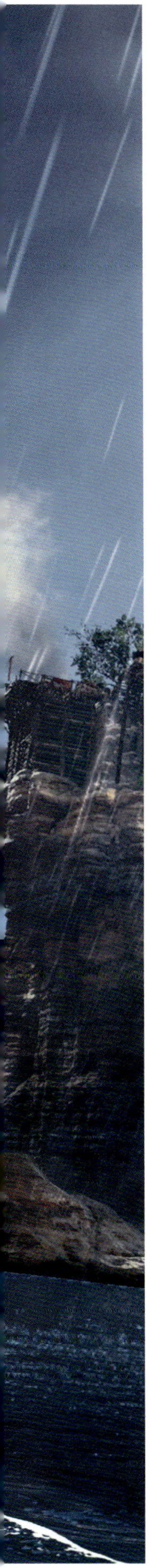

Langskip

The success of Viking raids, trade, and exploration relied heavily on their exceptional skill as shipbuilders and sailors. The Viking warship was the *langskip*, a long, slender vessel propelled by oars and sail.

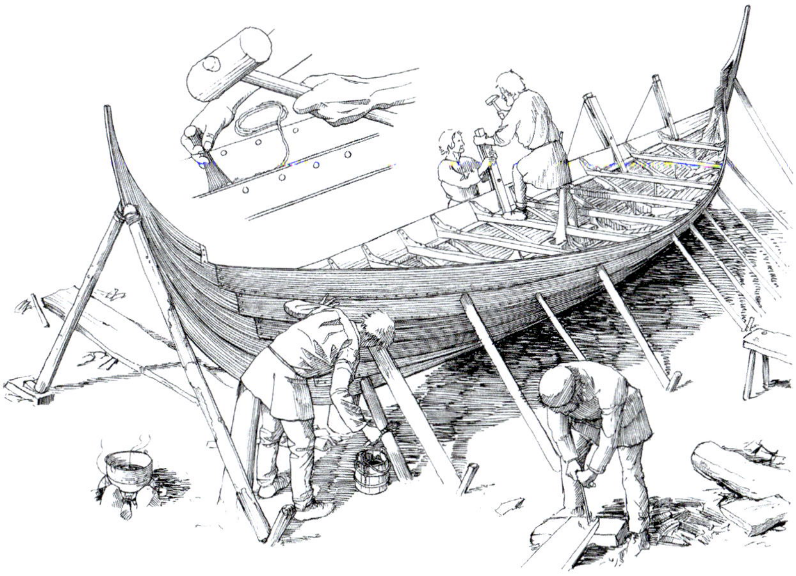

1. Assembly

Skilled artisans knew how to select the right trees and use their shape to best advantage. The spine of the ship was the sturdy and straight keel. To this were fixed the tall, wide bow and stern. Next, the hull planks were added and lastly the ribs and thwarts.

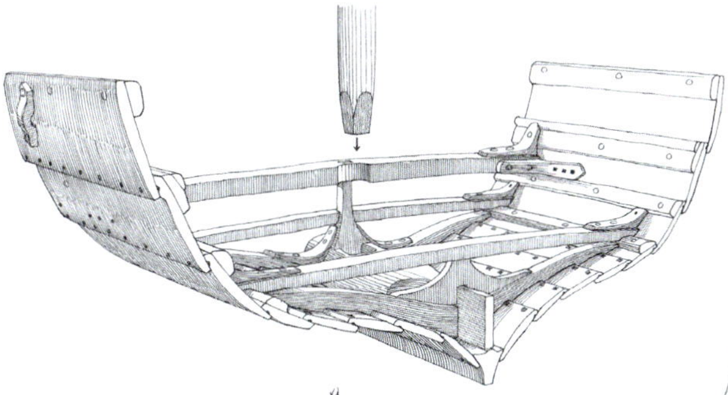

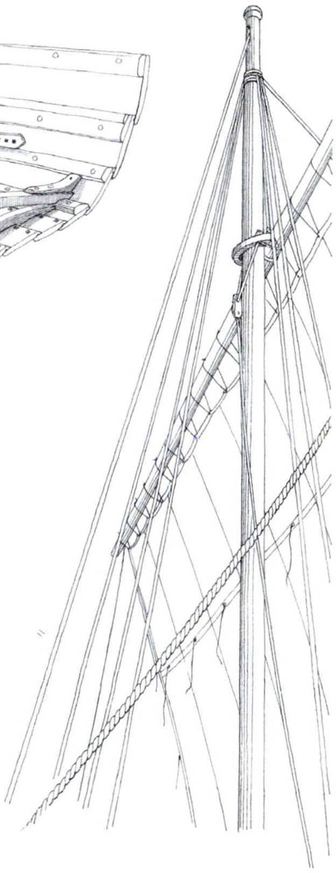

2. The mast

Building the mast and its sail and cordage also required expert skill and could cost as much as the ship itself.

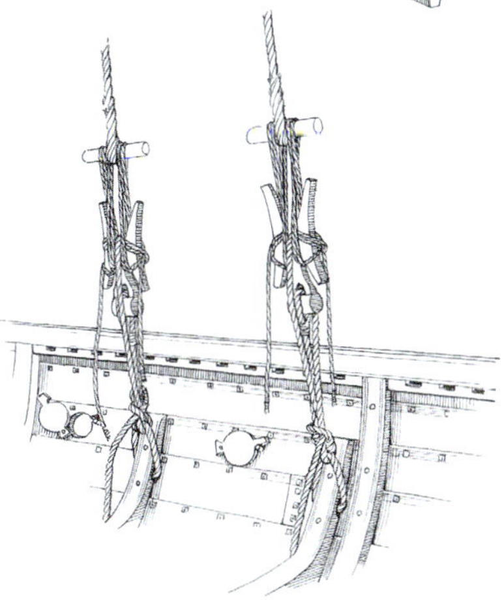

3. The sails

The Norse began using sails in the early 8th century. Made of wool and waterproofed with beef fat and ochre, their shape allowed for sailing into the wind, but it remained a difficult maneuver.

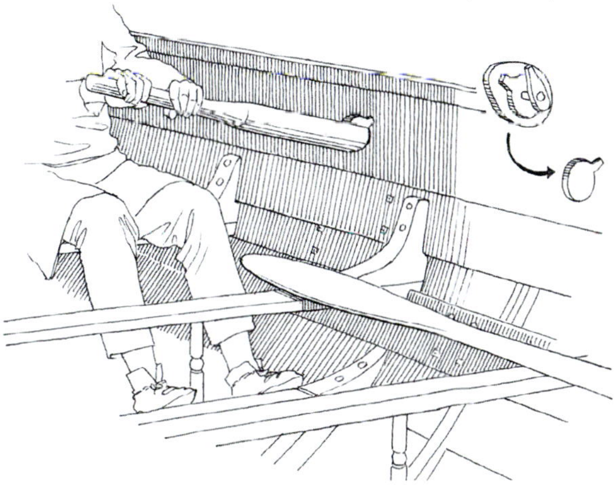

4. The oars

Placed in holes in the sides of the vessel, oars could be easily removed as needed.

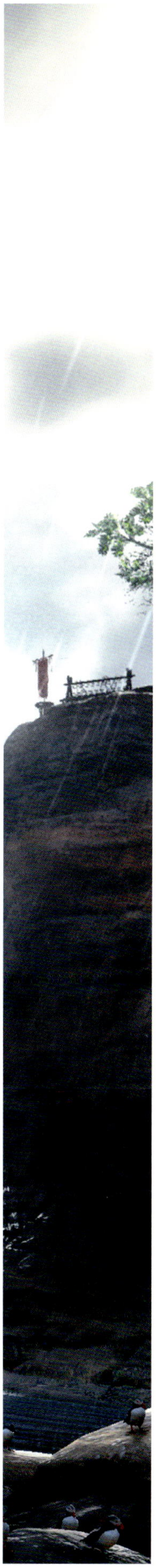

VINLAND AND L'ANSE AUX MEADOWS

Birgitta Wallace, archaeologist, specialist of the L'Anse aux Meadows site

It was the year 1021 according to the new Christian time reckoning. A group of men were working on a wooden dinghy set up outside a large building on a low terrace. A couple of boards and some floor planks were removed and replaced with newly cut ones. The scrap fell to the ground and some of it was thrown into a swampy area next to the terrace.

One thousand years later the scraps were retrieved from that swamp by archaeologists exploring evidence of a Norse presence in North America. The site was L'Anse aux Meadows on the shore of Epaves Bay on the Strait of Belle Isle, the northern tip of Newfoundland. It included the remains of eight buildings in 11th-century Icelandic-Greenland style, with turf walls and roofs supported by a wooden frame. Three of the buildings were large halls capable of housing close to 30 people each. Four were humbler dwellings of the kind used by domestics, and one was a dug-out hut where iron was produced.

Artifacts indicate that most of the Norse were men who performed heavy work such as carpentry, boat repair, iron making, and smithing. A spindle whorl and a needle hone tell that a few women were there, but there is no evidence of regular family life.

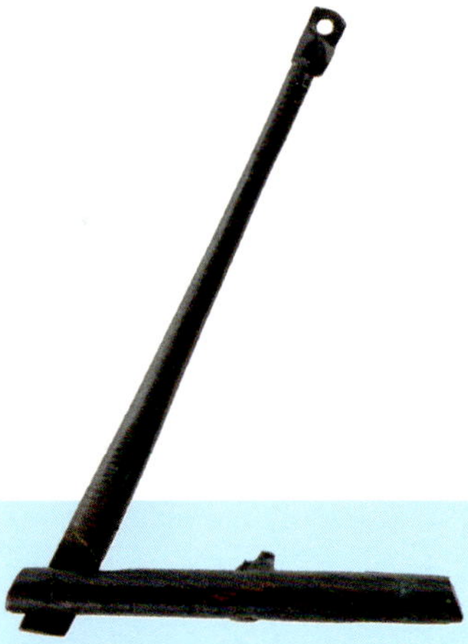

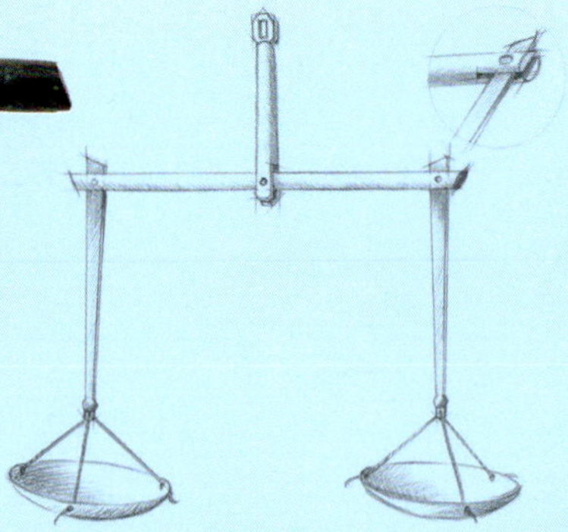

Scale

Remus Creek site,
Ellesmere Island, Nunavut.
Bronze. 14th century.
Canadian Museum of History.

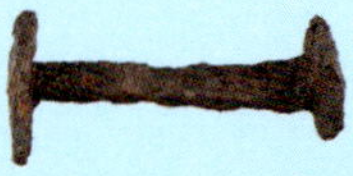

Ship rivet

Skraeling Island, Nunavut.
Iron. C. 1200.
Canadian Museum of History.

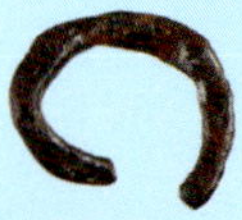

Chain mail ring

From an Indigenous house
dated from about 1190.
Skraeling Island, Nunavut.
Iron. Canadian Museum of History.

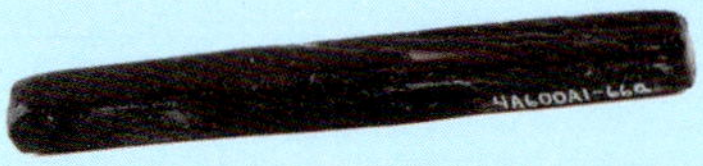

Whetstone

L'Anse aux Meadows.
Quartzite. C. 1021.
The Rooms Corporation
of Newfoundland and
Labrador, Provincial
Museum Division.

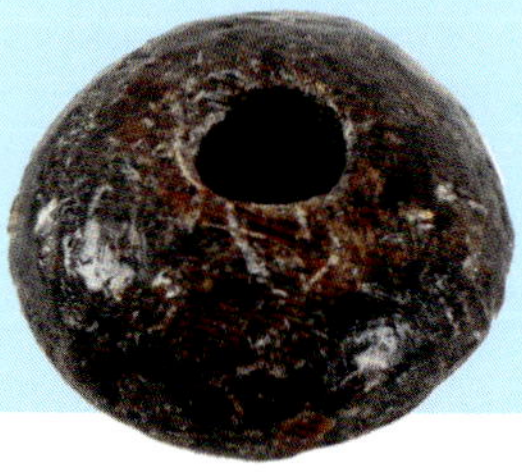

Spindle whorl

L'Anse aux Meadows.
Soapstone. C. 1021.
The Rooms Corporation of
Newfoundland and Labrador,
Provincial Museum Division.

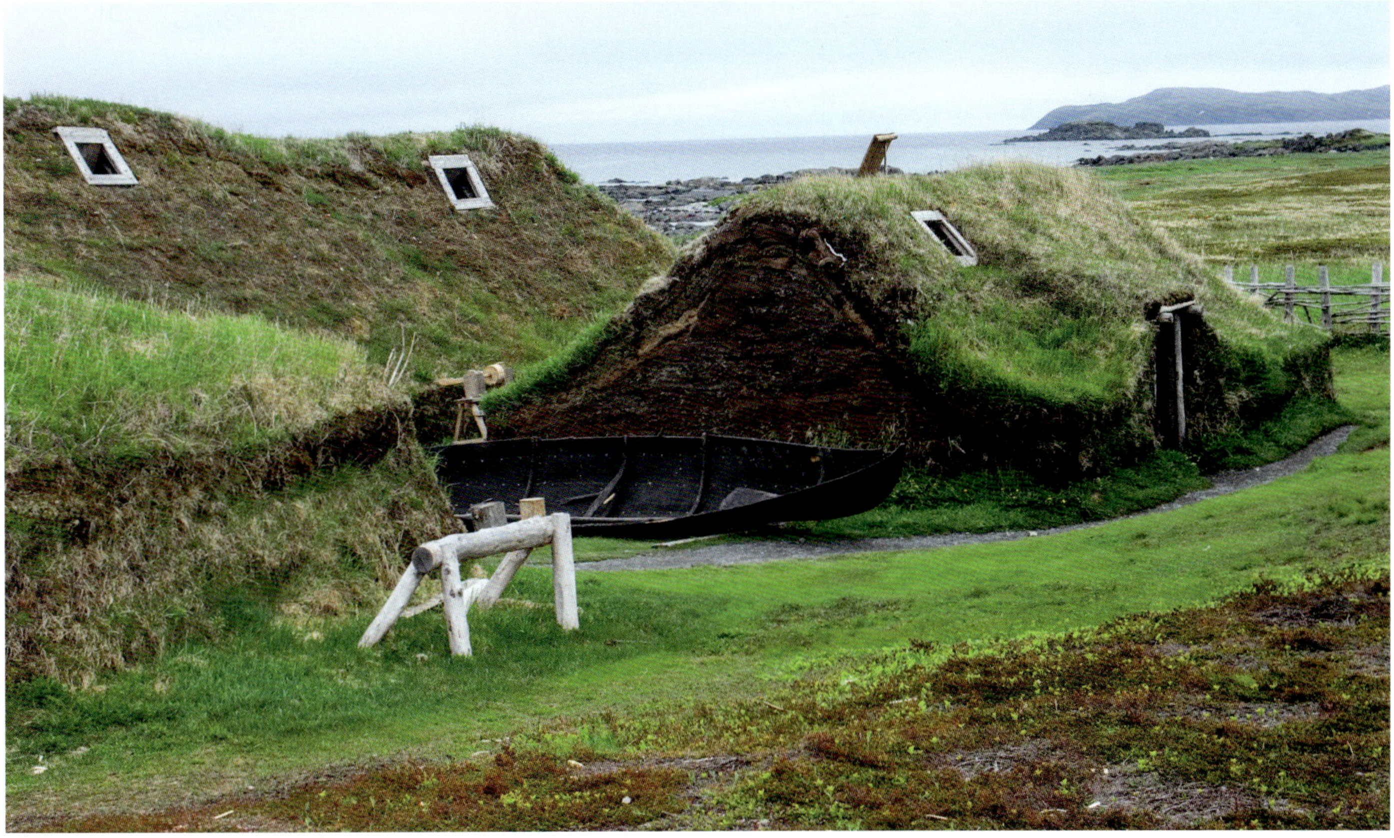

The buildings were solid and well-built, meant to last a long time. However, the archaeological excavation revealed that settlement was short, just a few years. A new method combining radiocarbon dating and dendrochronology revealed that in CE 1021, wood was being cut and dumped into the L'Anse aux Meadows bog. We do not know how long before and after 1021 the site existed, but the archaeological data indicate that it was not long on either side.

So how does L'Anse aux Meadows relate to the Vinland sagas? There is little doubt that L'Anse aux Meadows responds to Erik the Red's Straumfjörður in all aspects of type of settlement, type of participants, activities, and even landscape. Erik the Red's Saga places Straumfjörður in northern Vinland. It also has a southern outpost called Hóp where they found grapes and quality lumber. Evidence at L'Anse aux Meadows indicated that the inhabitants had visited more southern areas where grapes grew wild and lumber such as linden, white ash, and eastern white cedar could be harvested. This Hóp was almost certainly in the Miramichi and Chaleur Bay in New Brunswick.

Why was L'Anse aux Meadows abandoned so soon? Were there other sites? L'Anse aux Meadows and Vinland were far away from Greenland, almost as far as Norway, and the voyage was more difficult and dangerous. Vinland was also already settled, and the Norse feared the inhabitants, who outnumbered them. Most importantantly, the new colony in Greenland did not have enough workers to mount dangerous expeditions for resources they could get more easily from Europe. The colony was new, only around 400 settlers to work the farms that supported them all. The security of voyages to Europe for goods they themselves could not produce outweighed the need for dangerous voyages to Vinland. The Vinland adventure was ended. ■

ABOVE
L'Anse aux Meadows National Historic Site, Newfoundland.

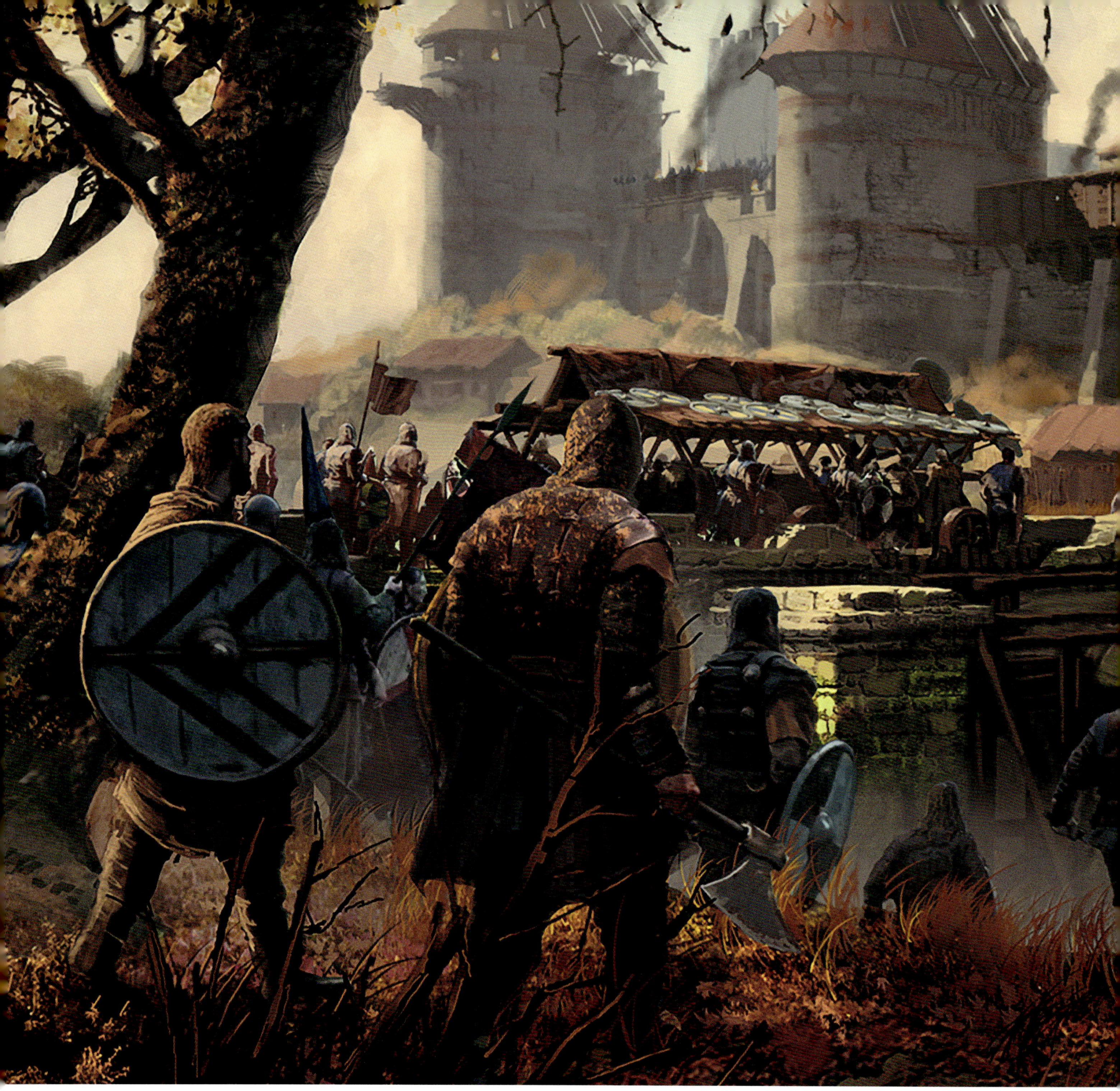

Surprising strategies, singular weapons

FORMIDABLE WARRIORS

Marc Carrier, historian

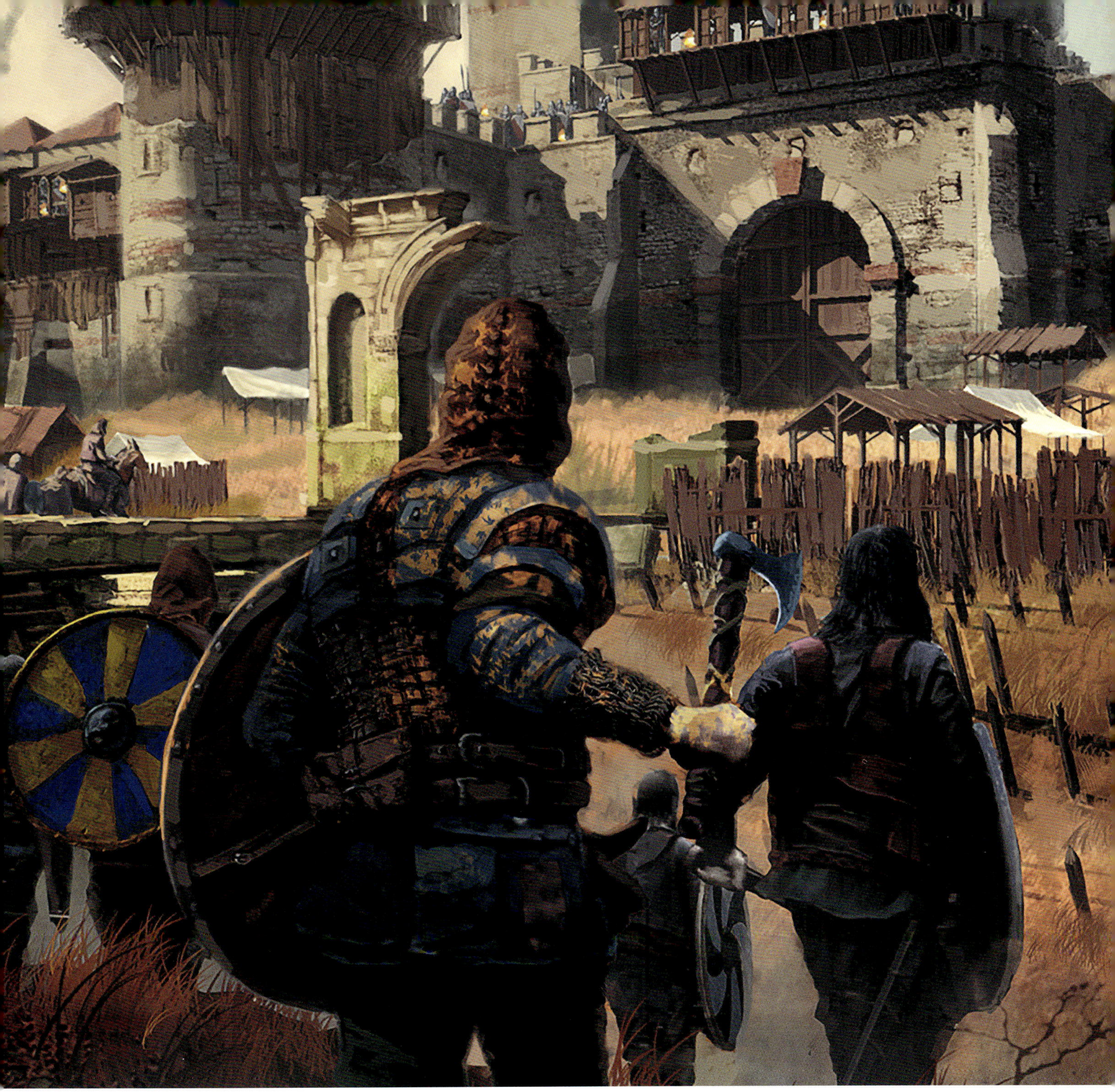

Despite popular belief to the contrary, the Vikings were not particularly more violent than other European peoples. The Middle Ages was a period that favoured opportunistic individuals and groups, whether that opportunism came in the form of cunning or force. And while the Vikings did gain a reputation for being formidable and terrifying warriors, this was primarily because their success as raiders, their military strategies, and their unusual weaponry truly captured the imagination of their contemporaries.

Vikings were attacking coastal regions of Western Europe by the 8th and 9th centuries. Their vessels were designed for speed and precision, allowing them to make lightning raids. Although built for the open ocean, Viking ships were flat-bottomed with shallow draughts, so they could sail up rivers and inlets and easily land on beaches, like

ABOVE
Art by Eddie Bennoun.
Assassin's Creed® Valhalla – TM&Copyright © Ubisoft Entertainment.

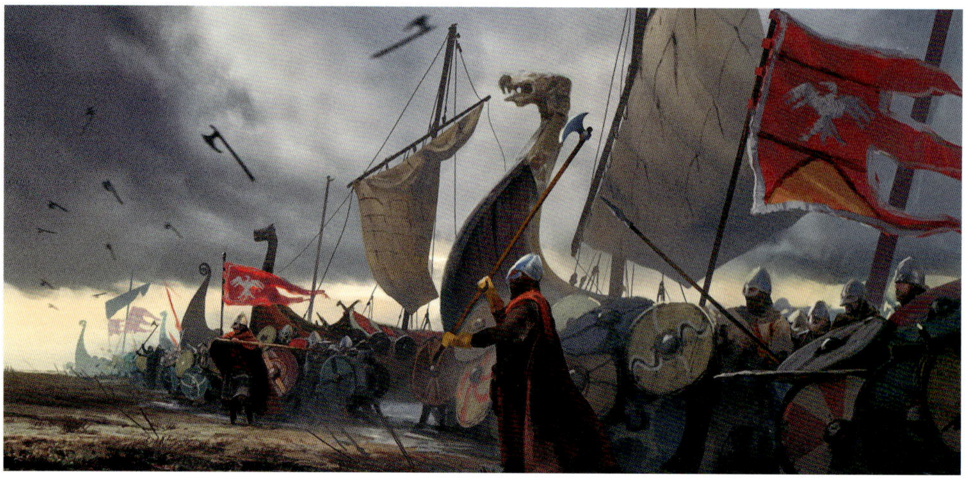

RIGHT
Art by Martin Deschambault.
Assassin's Creed® Valhalla – TM&Copyright © Ubisoft Entertainment.

rowboats. But they were also double ended, with symmetrical bows and sterns that gave them the ability to sail both backward and forward, meaning that after a raid, Viking ships could immediately be relaunched without having to turn around. Consequently, no one was safe from the Vikings' surprise, swift, and surgical attacks.

Fast, efficient raids

A typical raid might involve 150 to 500 Viking warriors, distributed among three to ten ships. Boys of 12 years or older could take part, and women were also eligible to fight. In Norse mythology, young female warriors with shields were called skyaldmö in Old Norse, or "shield maidens."

Armed with lances, axes, or swords, Vikings attacked monasteries and villages, seeking quick and easy plunder. Some Viking warriors wielded famous "Ulfberht swords," which were considered indestructible and struck terror in their enemies. For defence, they preferred shields made of softwood, which were more flexible, less brittle, and might jam an attacking weapon, allowing opponents to be more easily disarmed. Viking helmets were rounded and made of leather rather than metal—and they never had horns!

Viking raids tended to be swift and efficient. The attackers were often gone even before the alarm could be sounded and help could arrive. But they did occasionally foray inland, engendering the possibility of pitched battles and fighting on a larger scale. When confronted, Vikings often formed a triangular attack formation, called a "wedge," in which the best fighters were situated at the corners or the tip of a fighting group, the better to pierce enemy lines. Another formation, this one defensive, consisted of a shield wall, in which warriors stood side by side and overlapped their shields to form an impenetrable barrier.

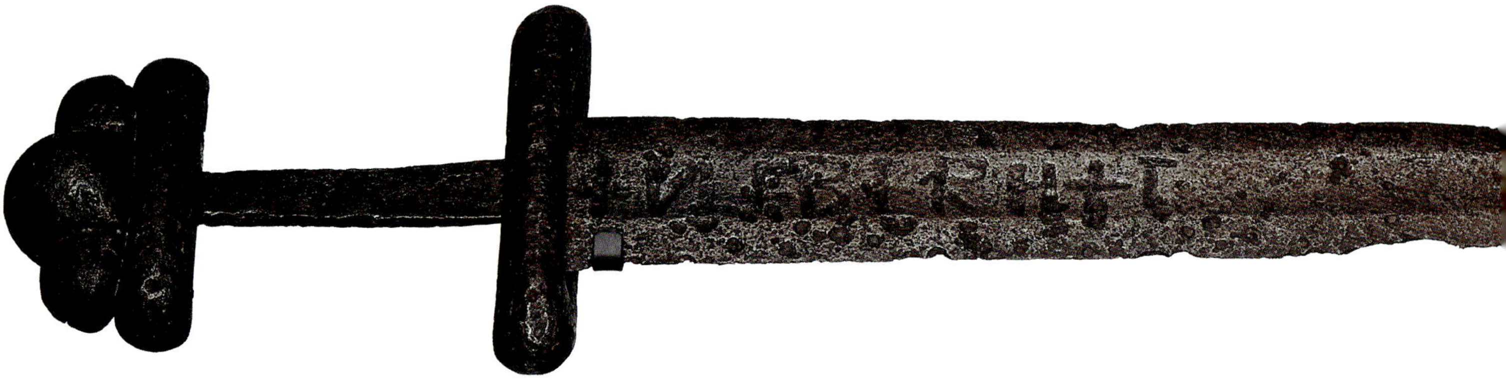

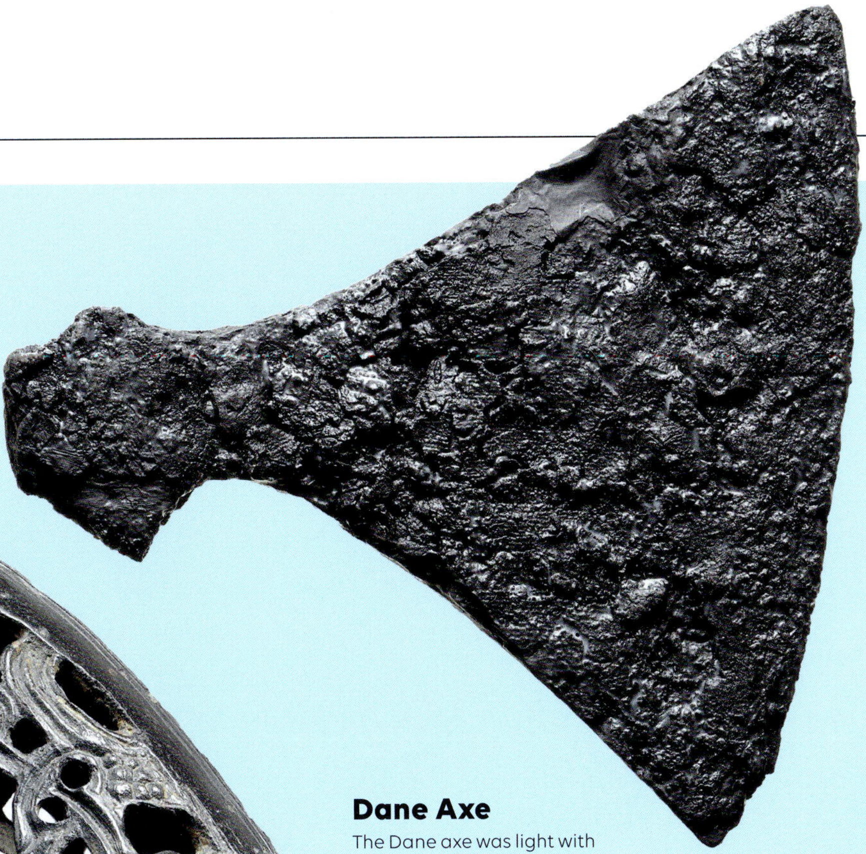

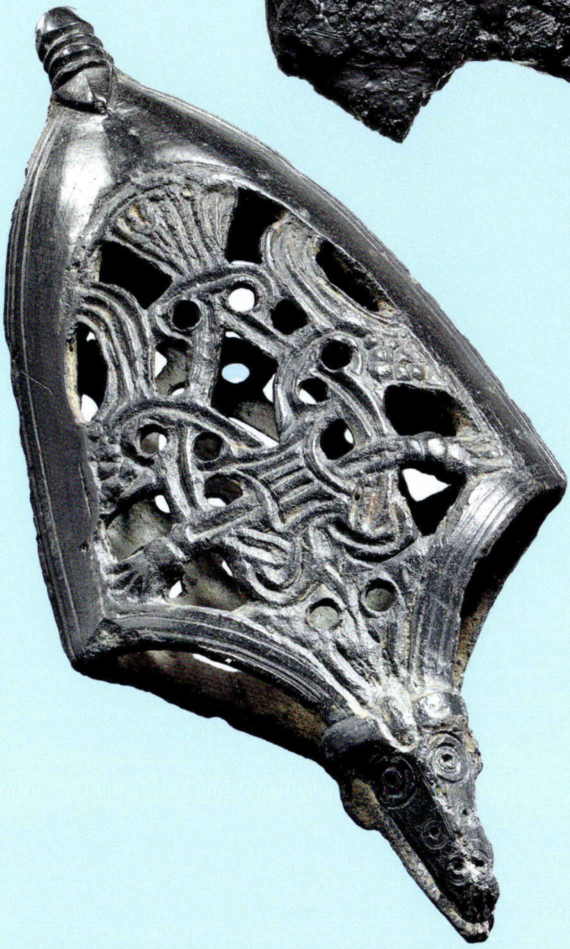

Dane Axe

The Dane axe was light with a wide blade and handle. The handle of a battle axe was usually over a meter long.

Iron. Hoby. 975–1050 CE.
National Museum of Denmark.

Sword chape

Great value was placed on swords. They were given names such as "Leg-biter" or "Blood-tongue." A scabbard chape is a piece of metal at the end of the scabbard, which was often lined with fur.

Bronze. Ballerup.
900–1000 CE.
National Museum of Denmark.

Ulfberht sword

Used by elite warriors, Ulfberht swords were forged from steel of a quality that was not reproduced in Europe before the turn of the 20th century. It is said that these swords are the first Western "brand name." Ulfberht was a known name and a guarantee of quality, though it was occasionally copied.

Crucible steel. Norway.
National Museum of Denmark.

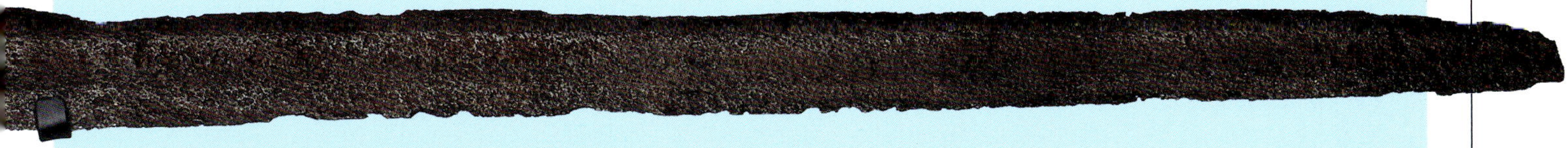

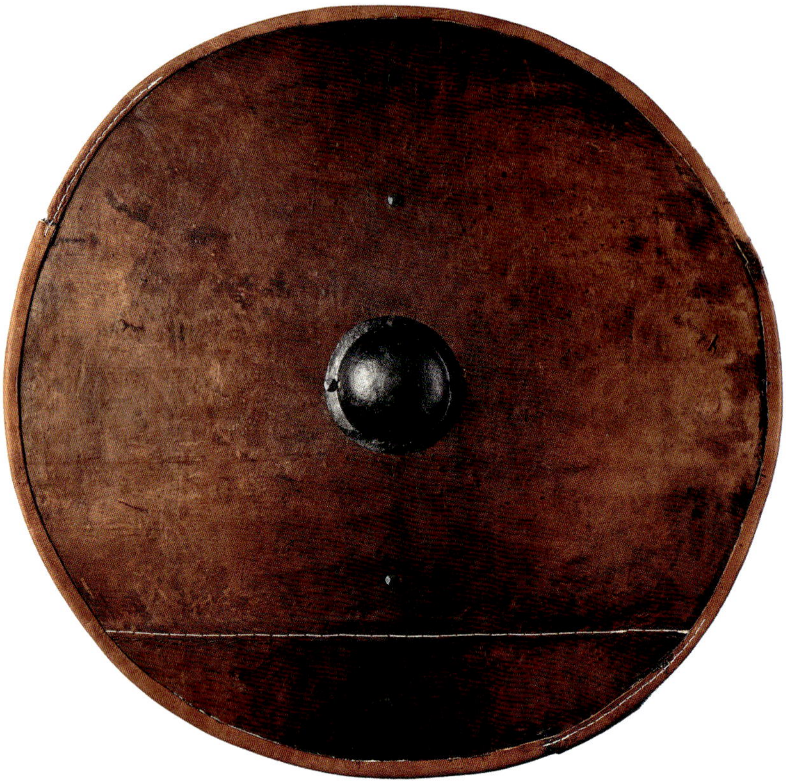

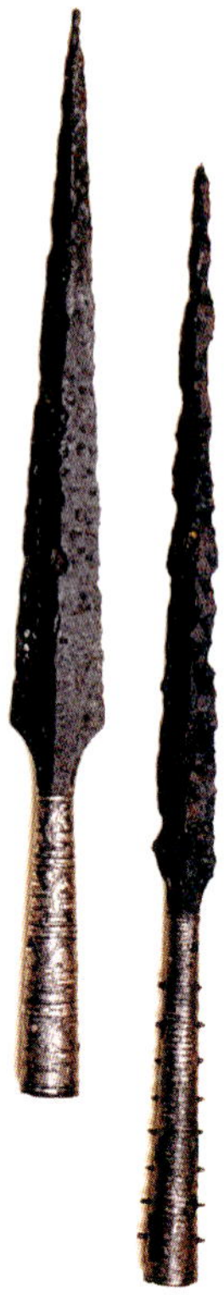

ABOVE LEFT
Viking shield.
Wood, metal.
Historiska museet, Stockholm.

ABOVE RIGHT
Viking spear tips.
Iron.
Historiska museet, Stockholm.

Vikings excelled at hand-to-hand combat; they were fierce and feared by opponents. Certain Viking warriors, called berserkers, were reputed to be able to enter a trance-like fury, characterized by screaming and rolled-back eyes, which made them immune to pain, ultra-powerful, and all-but invincible. The personal bodyguard of Scandinavian chieftains and kings was often made up of berserkers, generally in groups of 12 warriors.

Expeditions, conquests, settlements

When assembled for a land incursion or invasion, a Viking army might be several hundred and occasionally several thousand strong. The "Great Heathen Army," a Viking force from Denmark raised to invade England in the 9th century, may have been this large. The Anglo-Saxon king Alfred the Great, who ruled over Wessex in southern Great Britain, managed to halt the advance of this Viking army by winning the Battle of Edington in 878. The Anglo-Saxons' victory may have been in part due to their adoption of the Vikings' own shield-wall tactic.

As time went on and their opponents adapted to or imitated their strategies, the Vikings enjoyed fewer military successes. The last great battle of the Viking era, the Battle of Stamford Bridge, in 1066, is thought to have been lost by Norwegian king Harald Sigurdsson when his army was attacked by surprise and when his own shield wall collapsed against that of the English army.

But there is no doubt that the Vikings employed and imposed unconventional tactics for the day. They did not adhere to the principle of determining a battle's time and place beforehand, preferring to take their enemies by surprise and not deeming deception or trickery to be dishonourable. It was this pragmatism, combined with their skill and ferocity, that earned Vikings their reputation as formidable warriors, a reputation they enjoy to this day. ▮

The Vikings' military superiority waned when their opponents started using the same tactics

Working at the forge

Smiths contributed to all aspects of social life: they forged weapons, tools, nails for building, utensils, and decorative items. The smith garnered great respect in a Viking village. Some of the sagas honour the trade on an equal footing with explorers and warriors. The *Poetic Edda* recounts how the smith Völundr, imprisoned on an island with his hamstrings cut, escapes by flying away on wings that he has forged.

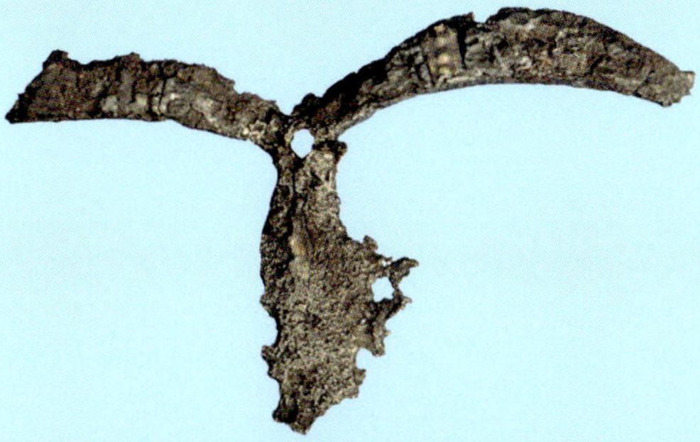

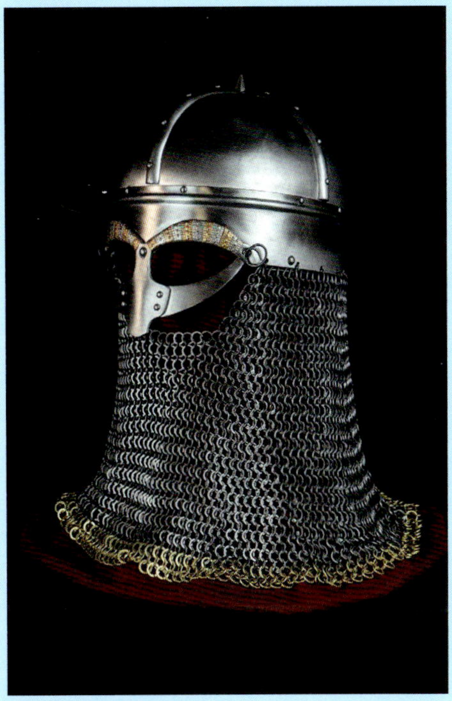

This fragment of a metal helmet from the Viking Age (left) is one of the rare in the world. Warriors generally wore leather helmets. This helmet fragment, part of the visor, was found in a chest which also contained blacksmith's tools (recreation on the right).

Iron. Tjele.
950–975 CE.

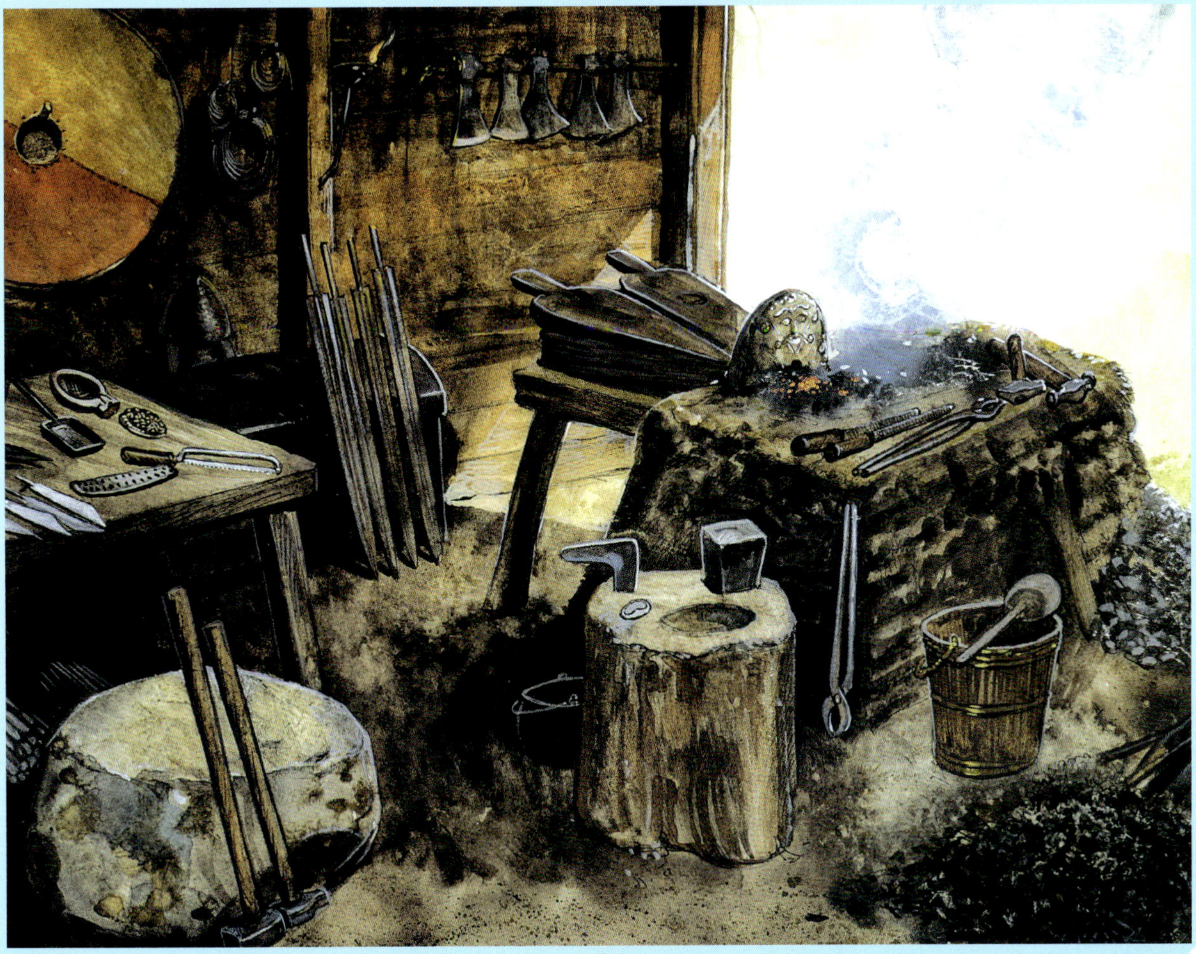

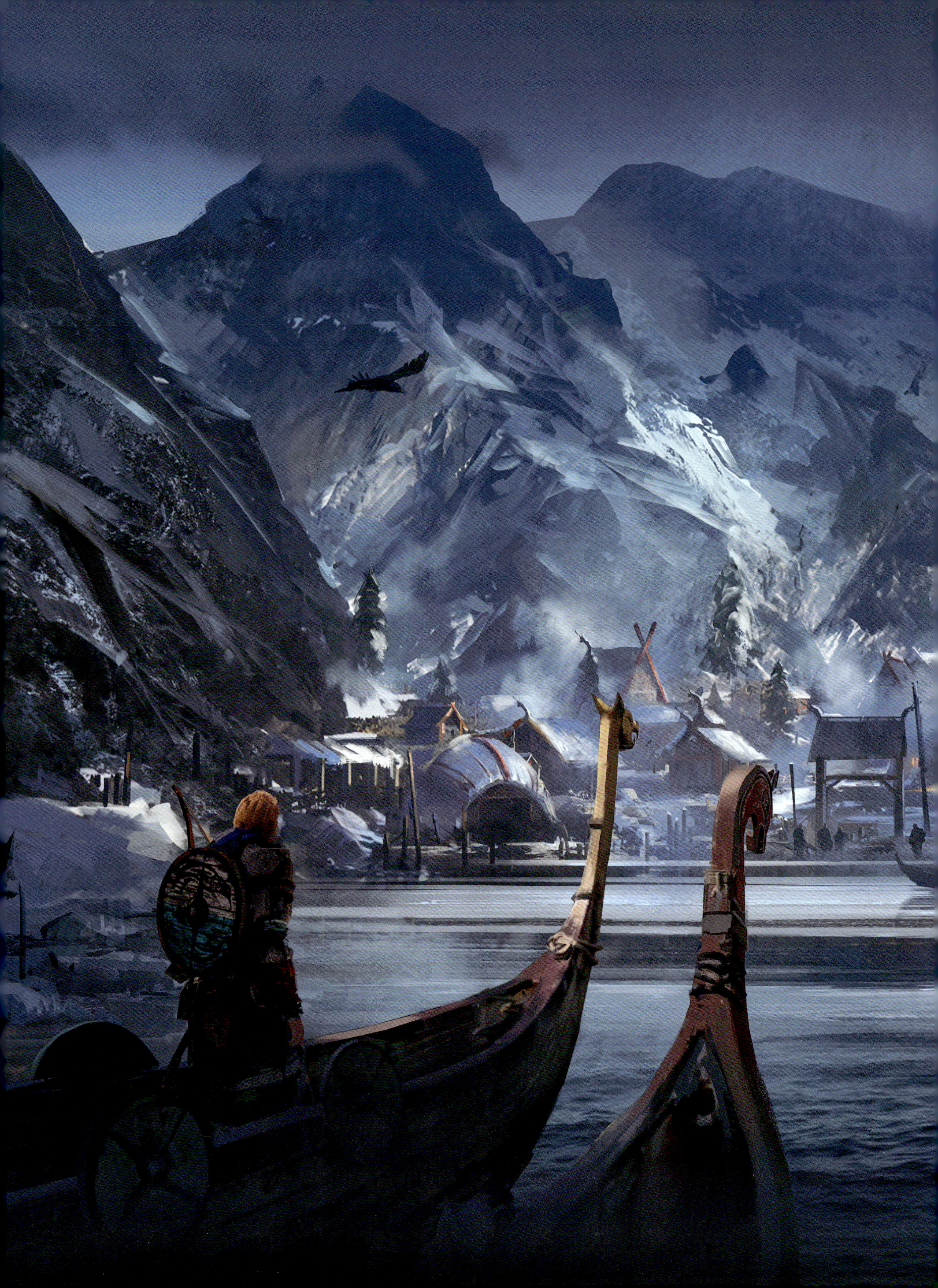

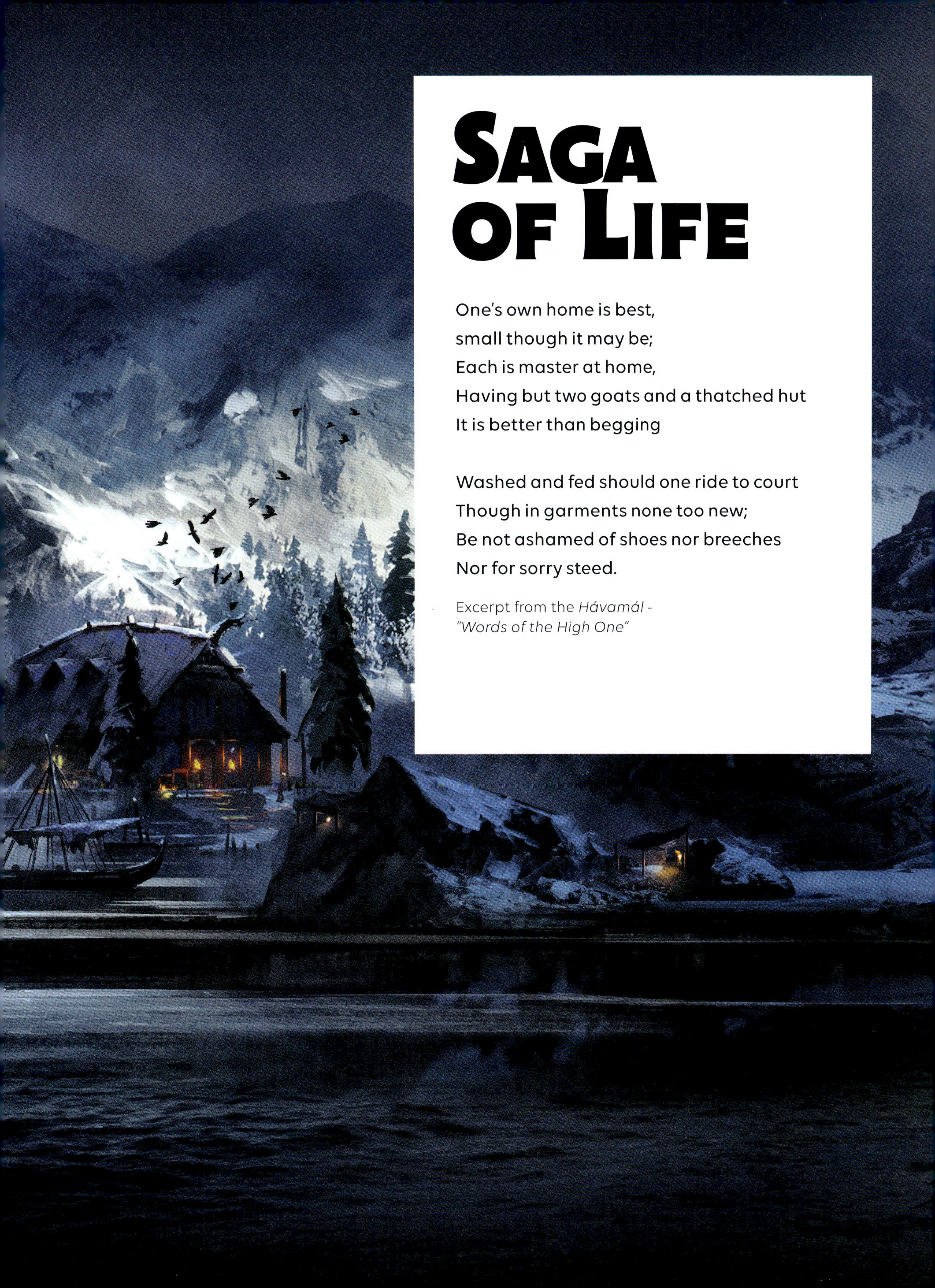

SAGA OF LIFE

One's own home is best,
small though it may be;
Each is master at home,
Having but two goats and a thatched hut
It is better than begging

Washed and fed should one ride to court
Though in garments none too new;
Be not ashamed of shoes nor breeches
Nor for sorry steed.

Excerpt from the *Hávamál* -
"Words of the High One"

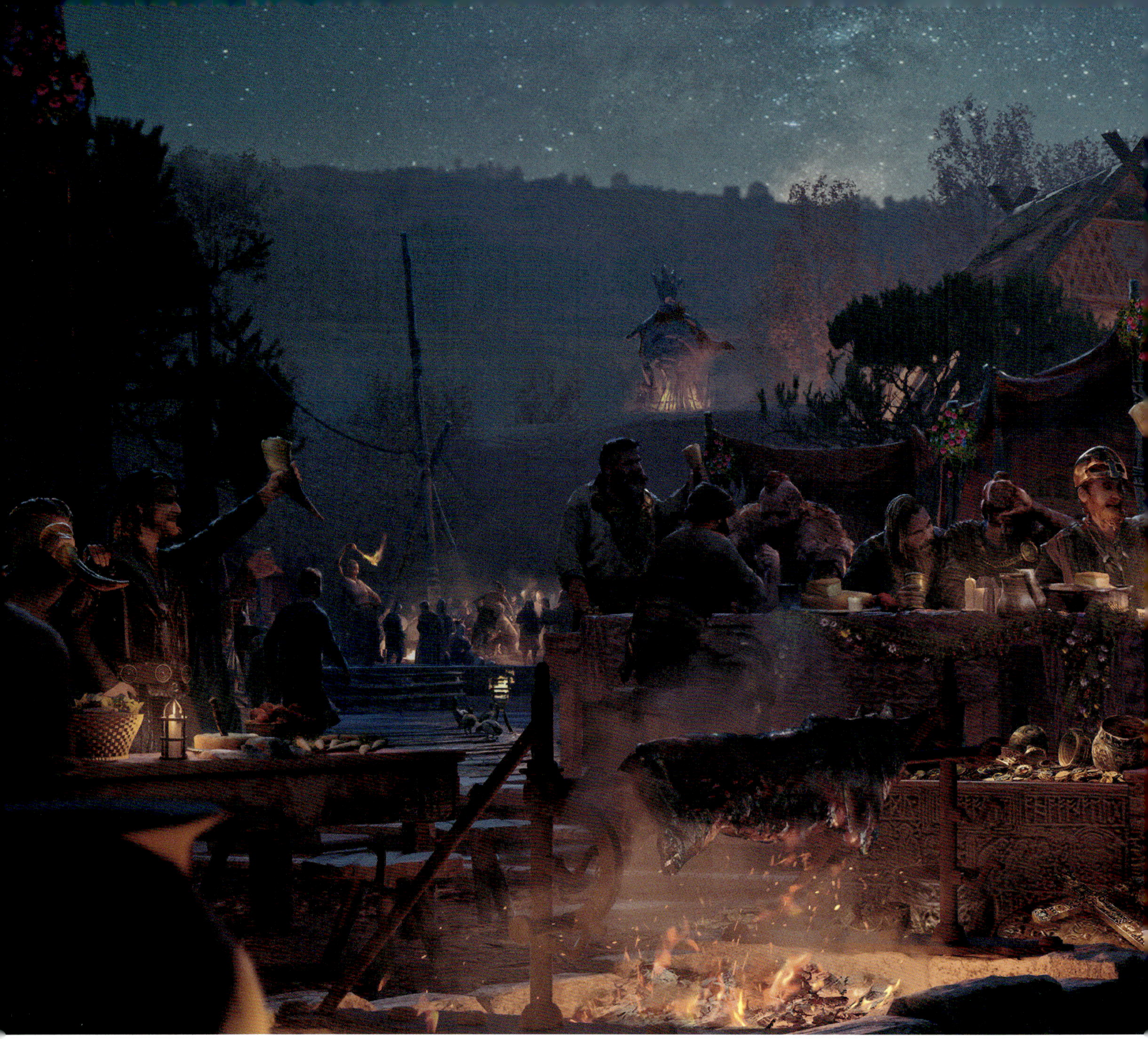

Daily life

A HIERARCHICAL SOCIETY

Peter Pentz, curator at the National Museum of Denmark

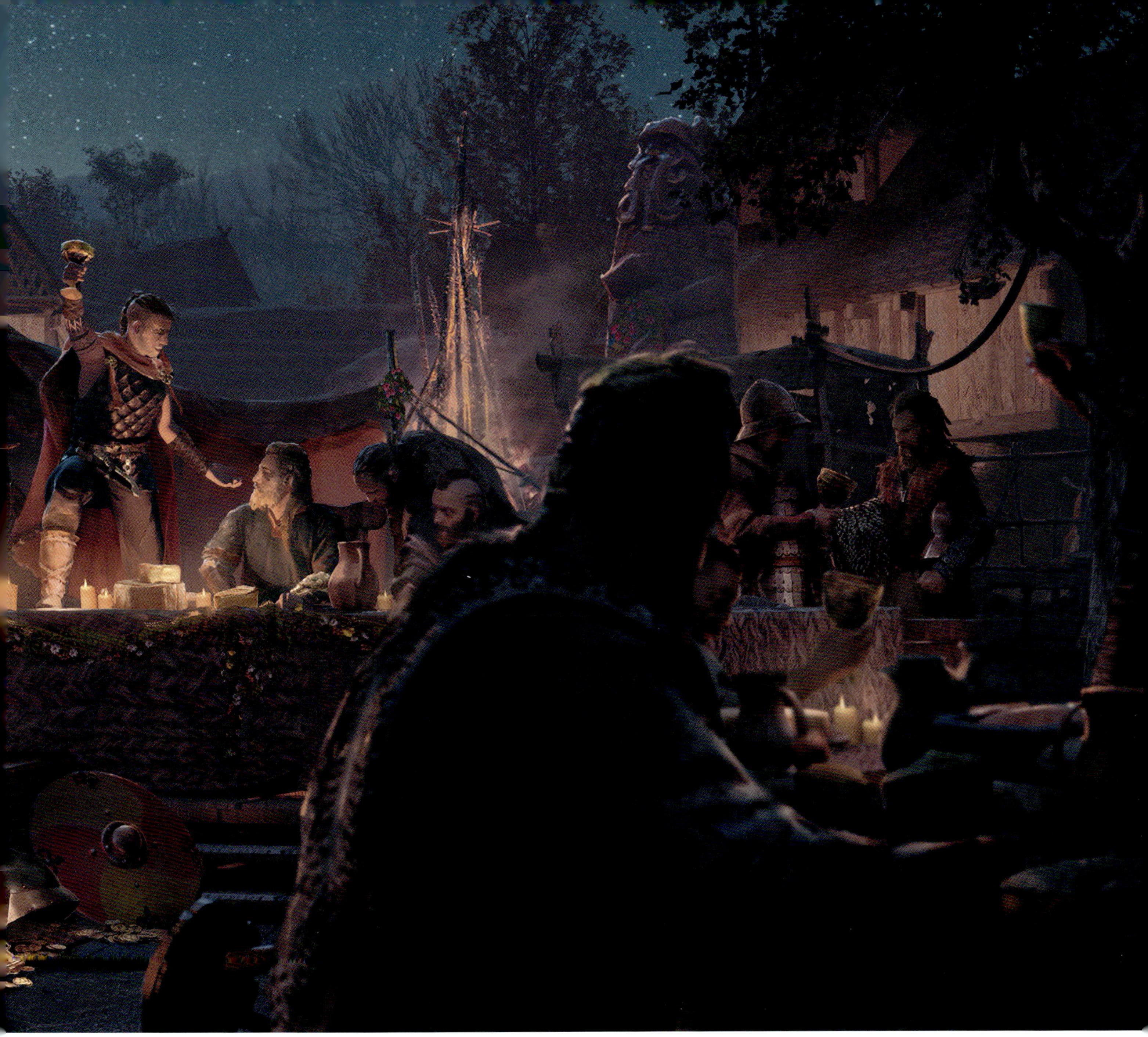

Games, martial arts, and work helped to teach children about life in Viking society. By the time they were 12 to 15 years old, children were regarded as adults, but, naturally, without the experience and knowledge of older people. Marriages were arranged early, sometimes when those involved were still quite young children. Even though poetry from the Viking Age, and especially sagas, are rich with tales of love and sex, marriage was a way to form bonds—not just between the betrothed, but even more so between the two families.

Women who were married to farm owners had an important role as a kind of manager. The housewife on a farm had keys to the locks and cupboards—these types of keys have been found in the graves of many women, hanging from a belt or a chain on the deceased. One of the early medieval laws with its origins in the Viking Age states that if a man's lover had command over the keys to locks and fastenings and shared a table and bed with the man over three winters, then the only thing he was lacking to make her his wife!

ABOVE
Art by William Koh.
Assassin's Creed® Valhalla – TM&Copyright © Ubisoft Entertainment.

PREVIOUS DOUBLE PAGE
Art by Donglu Yu.
Assassin's Creed® Valhalla – TM&Copyright © Ubisoft Entertainment.

The young men who didn't inherit farms had to work as farmhands. Some chose to go the way of war, maybe they joined the local chieftain's longship on a Viking raid. For many of those who headed out and settled somewhere else, the possibility of owning land was surely tempting.

Occupying the lowest rank in society were the enslaved people. It is certainly not their possessions that archaeologists find in excavations and the enslaved are almost invisible in the written sources and archaeology. It is very rare to find an "unfree" named on the runestones.

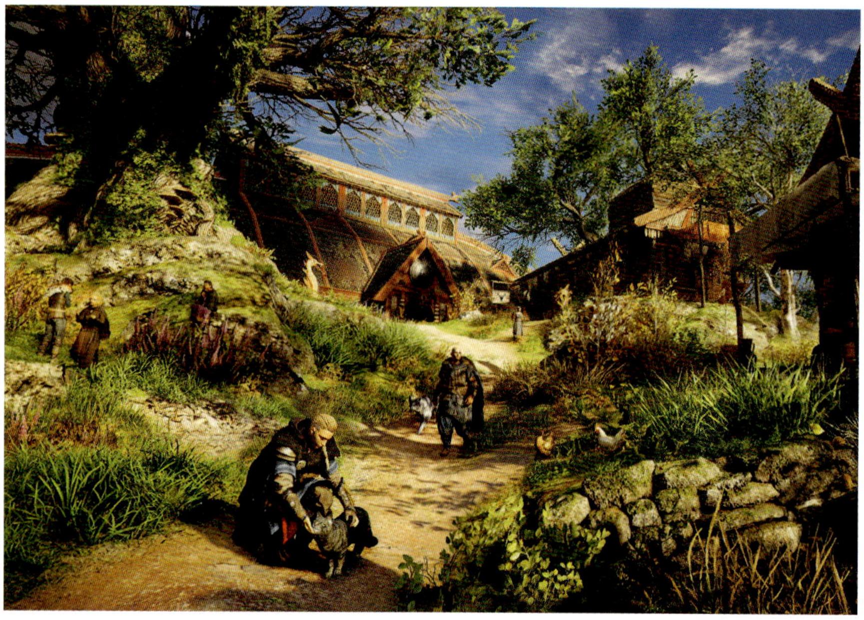

Enslaved and captives of the Vikings could take on positions of trust, but most of them were occupied with working in the fields

It is, however, also understood that the enslaved could achieve a respectable place in society. A child of an Icelandic father and an enslaved woman could, for instance, grow up as a free child. Many of the sagas take place in Iceland and from them it is evident that many enslaved persons came from Ireland. Modern genetic studies have confirmed this.

But, of course, it was not only in Iceland, that slavery contributed to the economy. The Vikings enslaved people from France, England, Ireland and other countries. Their fellow Scandinavians could also be enslaved. We do not have sufficient records to be able to ascertain just how many of the Vikings enslaved and brought back to Scandinavia. Some of the people who were captured were taken as hostages and were later released. The majority, however, were certainly sold on to other places in the Vikings' large network.

Occasionally, an archaeologist will stumble upon a grave containing a lord or noblewoman buried together with a person who was killed specifically for that purpose. Supported by both written sources and modern scientific analysis, archaeologists have identified the victims as enslaved persons.

The enslaved and captives of the Vikings were essentially valued for their labour, or as a hostage or trade item. Even though an unfree could take on positions of trust, such as householder or maybe even as a warrior in the king's army, most of the enslaved persons were occupied with working in the fields as shepherds and with other kinds of farm work. The greatest divide in Viking society wasn't between men and women, nor was it between children and adults, it was the gulf between the free and unfree.

ABOVE

Illustration from Assassin's Creed® Valhalla.

Sport and leisure

Many of the things that we consider to be leisure activities today were regarded by Vikings as sport. Sport covered many more activities than it does now. Apart from proper physical efforts, sport also included board games, poetry and music. Amongst the physical games, weapon games and archery were highly regarded. Wrestling, races, tug of war and

1

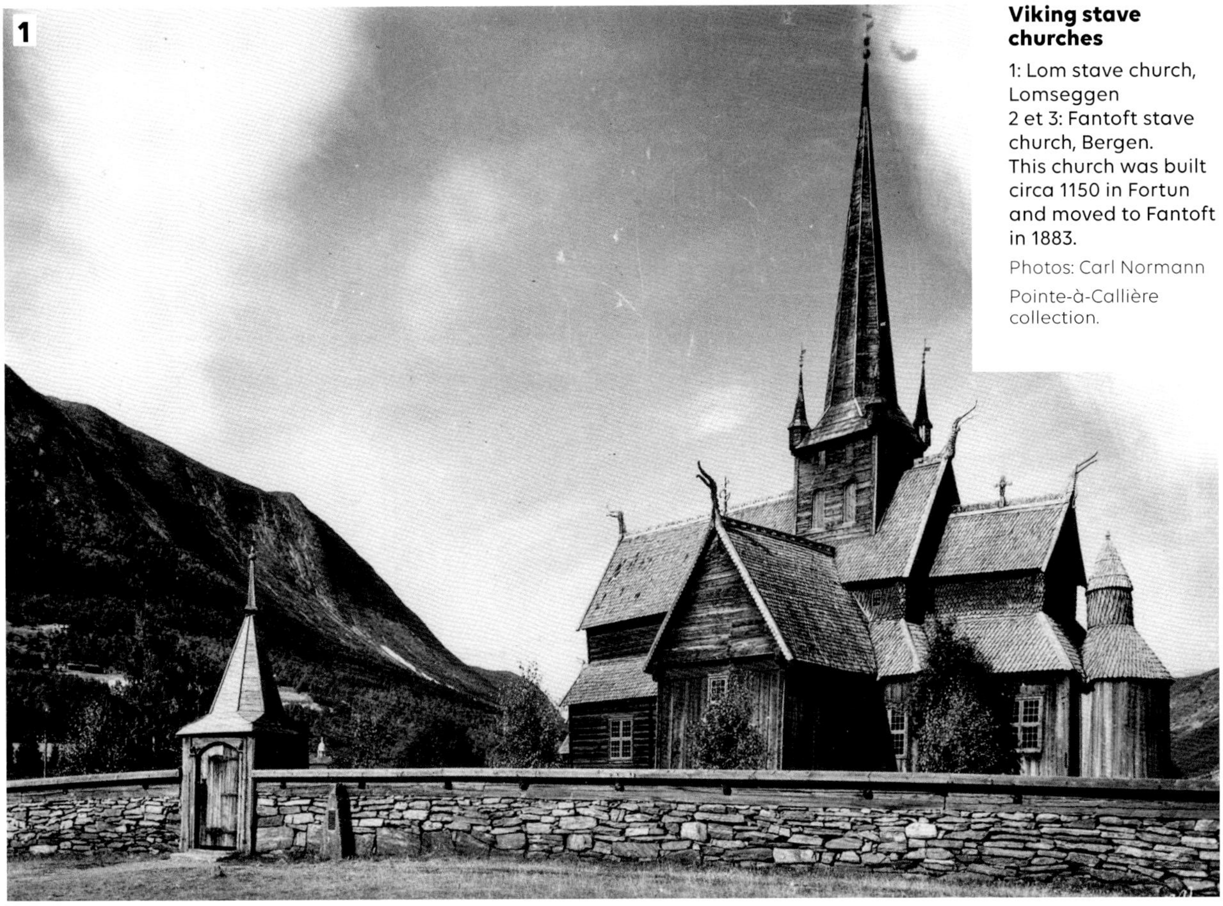

2

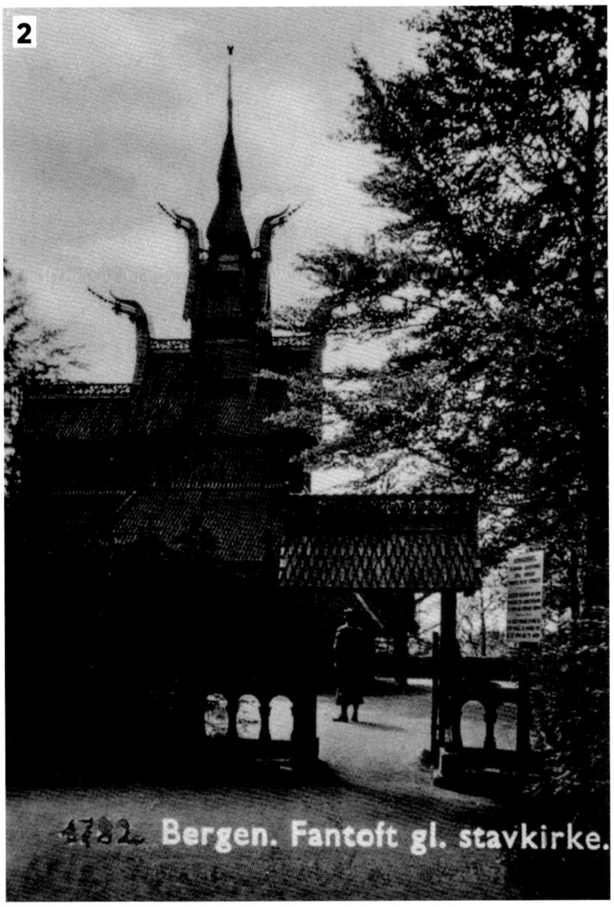

3

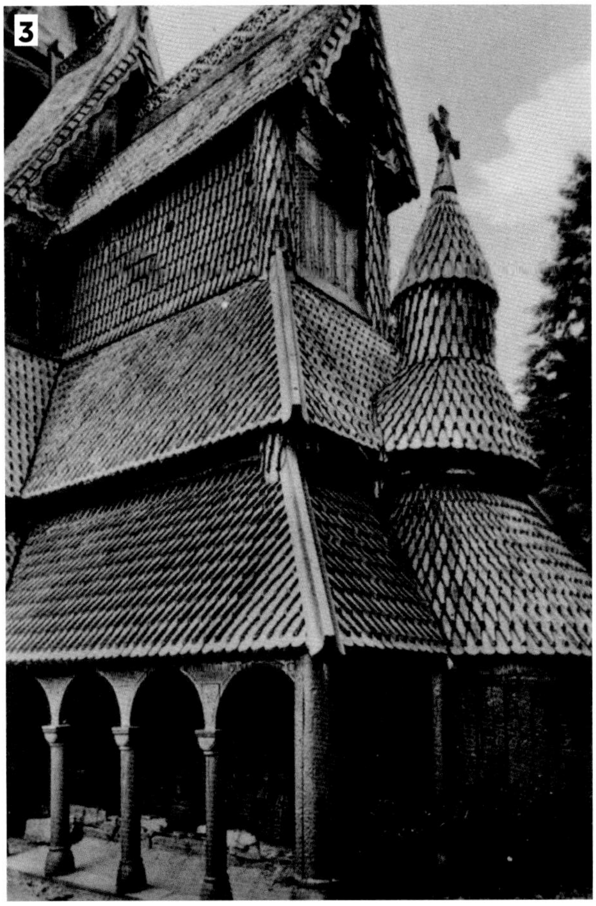

Viking stave churches

1: Lom stave church, Lomseggen
2 et 3: Fantoft stave church, Bergen.
This church was built circa 1150 in Fortun and moved to Fantoft in 1883.

Photos: Carl Normann

Pointe-à-Callière collection.

Jewellery
Wheel-shaped pendant.

Bronze. Bislev
National Museum of Denmark.

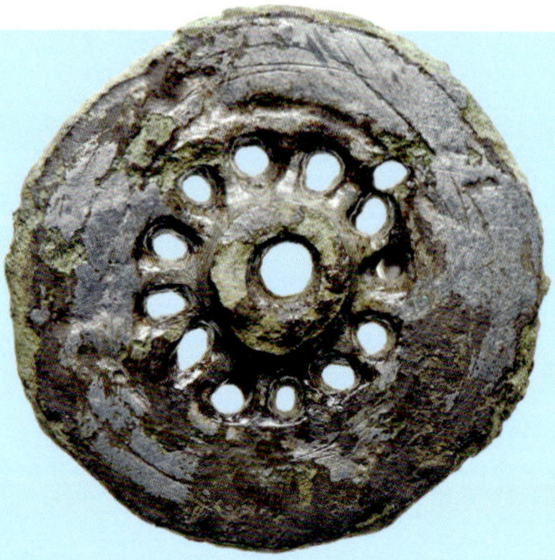

Comb
Vikings cared about hygiene and took care of their hair. They appreciated combs, which also helped get rid of lice.

Bone. Föhr, Germany.
800-900 CE.
National Museum of Denmark.

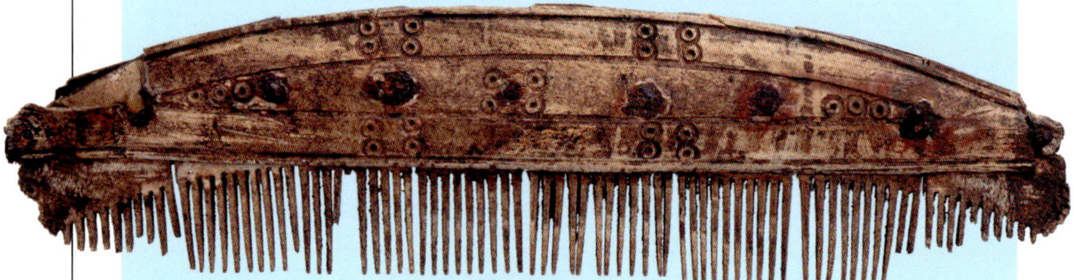

Utensil
Ornamented spoon.

Bone or antler.
Hovindsholm, Norway.
National Museum of Denmark.

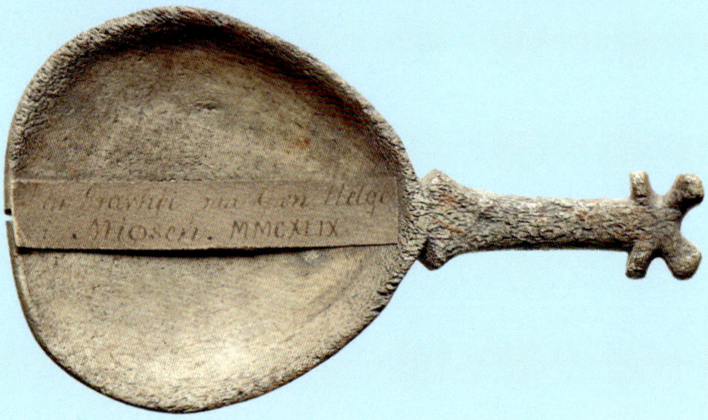

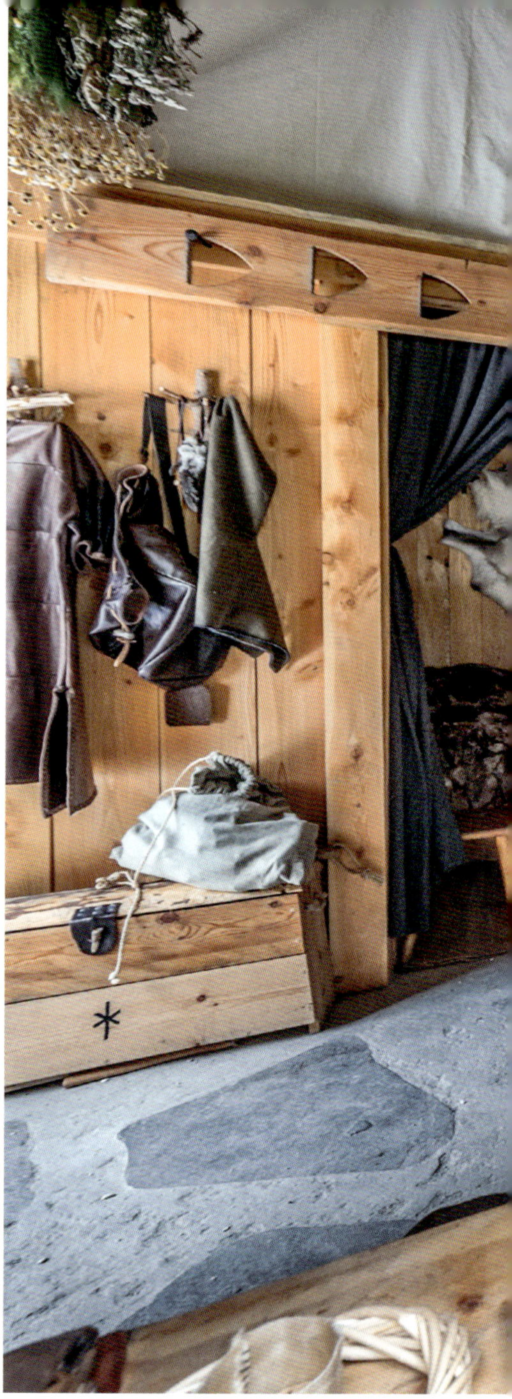

Viking poetry was far from primitive, it was image evoking and featured many ingenious metaphors

swimming battles—where opponents dunked each other under the water, were also sports that helped physical development. Ball games were played nearly all year round while ice-skating and skiing were, of course, mostly winter activities. Horse fighting, where two horse owners incited their stallions to attack each other, was a violent sport where blood flowed.

A very particular type of sport was practiced while sailing. With the longship barreling ahead at a good speed, thanks to the strokes of the oarsmen, the Vikings would jump from the stern to the closest oar and then run forward through the rows of heaving oars up to the bow, only to run the whole way back again along the other side of the ship. A couple of the Viking kings were particularly proficient at this game.

The main purpose of sport was probably to train youth for a life of battle and hunting, while the more restrained sports helped to develop and practice linguistic

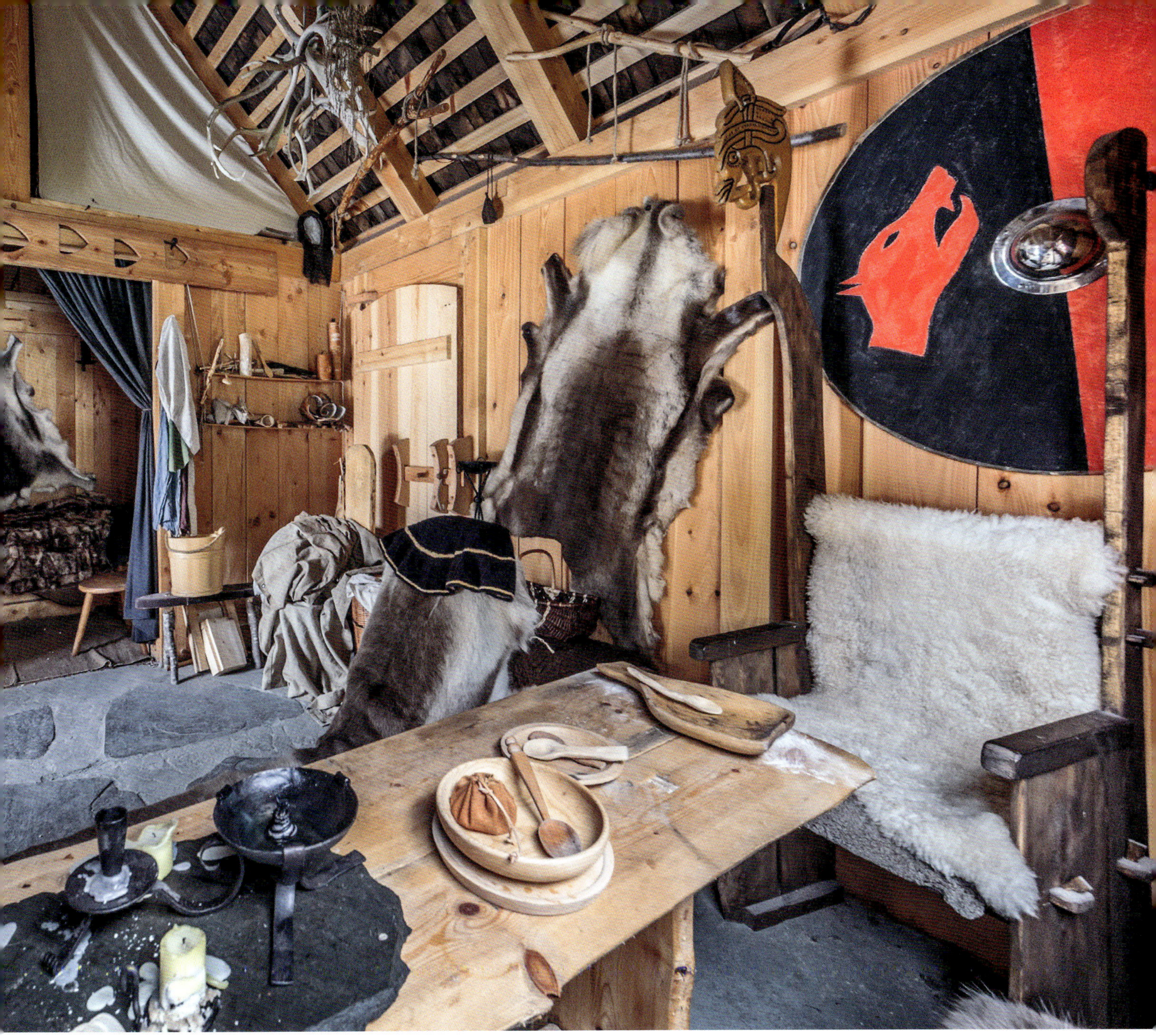

and social skills. Harps were probably mostly played in the halls of chieftains, while singing and playing flute instruments was something in which everyone could participate.

One source of entertainment at festive occasions was drinking competitions, with the aim of drinking your companions under the table. In the meantime, participants could take part in word-feuds, which were battles of wit and oratorical skills. If the later sources are to be believed, then playing with the knuckle bones left-over from meals was also a popular game.

The gift of the gab and linguistic ability seem to have been important for the Vikings. Viking poetry, which was mostly transcribed after the Viking Age, supports this. Contrary to what many people assume, Viking poetry was far from primitive, it was image evoking and featured many ingenious metaphors. And it was not just men who were clever poets. Much of the poetry originates from female skalds. Kings and chieftains also regularly threw themselves in bardic poetry, which they considered to be a sport, equal to games and athletics. ▮

ABOVE

Replica of the inside of a traditional Viking house.

Norway, Vestland county, Naeroyfjord, Aurland, Gudvangen.

Better off than most other European women of the day

Woman in the Viking Age

Michèle Hayeur Smith, Haffenreffer Museum of Antropology, Brown University

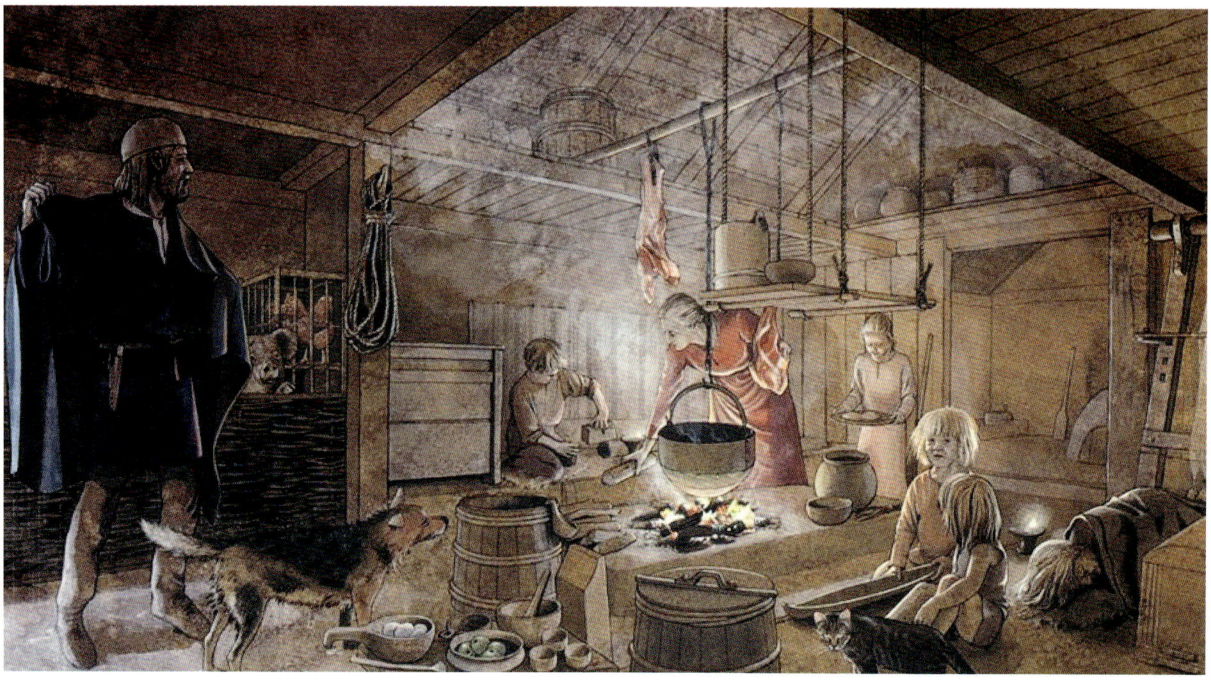

ABOVE

Recreation of the inside of a Viking house.

Drawing by Flemming Bau.

Viking Age women lived in a predominantly patriarchal society and were considered subordinate to men. Men held dominant public roles as heads of the family, political leaders, members of Viking expeditions, and were responsible for most cult activities, trade, etc.

Wealthy men in the Viking Age were polygamous, with one official wife and at times several concubines. Official wives had to make do with this arrangement but often found themselves in positions of power, controlling the activities of these women along with other householders and slaves. These official wives, known as the *husfreyja*—lady of the house, were often venerated for their skills and could temporarily take over male roles in trade and running farms, while their husbands were away on Viking expeditions.

Despite their seemingly subordinate social roles, women were better off than most of their European counterparts and held dominance over men in many areas of life, with considerable power. Viking Age extended families were crucial elements of society, both politically and economically. They were not only multi-generational but often included foster children, men bound through brotherhoods, and poor relatives. Decent was reckoned on both the mother's and father's sides and women generally maintained knowledge over their own lineages and their husbands' families. Using this knowledge, women could practice a considerable amount of power over their male kinsmen, goading them to seek revenge if the family's honor had been violated.

Women were also legally allowed to divorce if they were dissatisfied by their union. Late Viking Age law codes list situations in which women could legally seek a divorce, including if their husband dressed in female attire, was impotent and incapable of consummating the marriage, or killed his wife's brother. Women could only inherit land and wealth from their sons, not their fathers or husbands. On rare occasions they also inherited titles, such as the chieftaincy, but could only partially fulfill the role putting forth their grievances and agendas via male kinsmen even though they were not allowed to partake in legal or political assemblies.

Warriors or diviners

The burial of a woman fully equipped with weaponry and horses at the Swedish site of Birka suggests that some women may also have taken on roles as warriors, whether symbolically or in battle. In myths and sagas, women appear on the battlefield not only as supernatural Valkyries, but also as shieldmaidens and as practitioners of battle magic aimed at confusing the enemy. Women also performed a type of female magic called *seiðir* (a type of divination). This type of magic was connected with Freyja, a goddess of both love and war who collected half the dead warriors on the battlefield. The other half were taken by the Valkyries to Oðin in Valhalla.

Women wielded considerable power through their associations with female magic, not only *seiðir*, but also as part of textile production, which men avoided. It was thought that women were able to cast spells through weaving and spinning that could change the course of fate, bind people together, or potentially kill them. The sagas also suggest that women were involved in other crafts, as poets and skálds, possibly even as ship builders although information about these roles is sparse. Finally, women were deeply involved in planning, organizing, and successfully settling new colonies. ▮

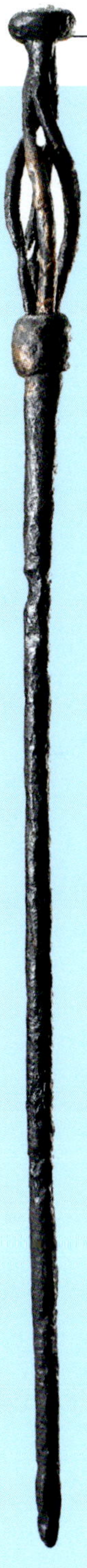

Völva's staff

Described in various mythological contexts, a *völva* was a seeress who could perform sorcery, enter trances, and foretell warriors' futures. They appear to have been actively involved in various religious functions. They carried wands (*völva* means "wand carrier" in Old Norse), though these did not appear to have any practical use. The wands' shape was inspired by the distaff, a tool used in spinning and weaving, itself a craft with significant magical connotations and associated with the goddess Freya.

Iron. Fuldby. 800–900 CE. National Museum of Denmark.

Key to the household

After marriage, the wife became the bearer of the key to the household. This symbolized her status as manager of the domain. The key was worn outside her clothes in order to be clearly visible.

Bronze. National Museum of Denmark.

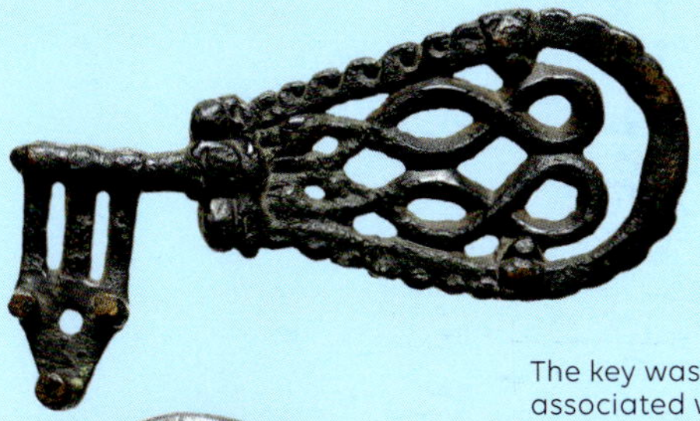

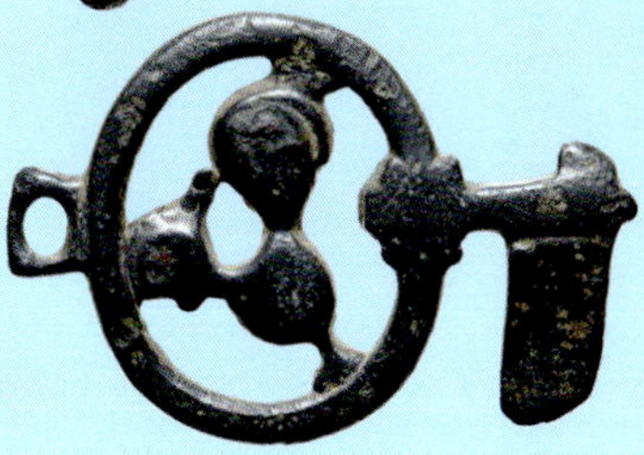

The key was often associated with Frigg, wife of Odin and goddess of the household and married women. This key with openwork circular handle contains a single animal.

Bronze. Tisvilde National Museum of Denmark.

Spindle whorl

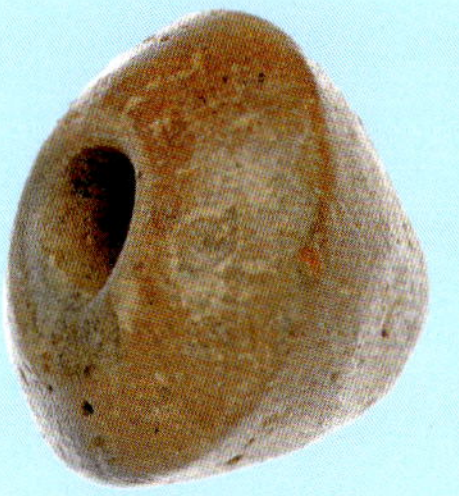

Often adorned with runes, mainly the owner's name, spindle whorls had both utilitarian and magical purposes, since they were also used to cast spells.

Amber. National Museum of Denmark.

UNPARALLELED ARTISANS

Craftspeople played a vital role in Viking culture and enjoyed high social status. They constructed ships, worked iron, and cast bronze. They produced fine jewellery, leather goods, textiles, combs, and glass beads.
The sophistication of their work was made possible thanks to the Vikings' extensive trade network, which gave them access to a range of high-quality materials, specialized tools, and the most advanced technology.
The Vikings built sites specifically to produce jewellery and adornments. Among their most beautiful objects, intricately decorated brooches conveyed the wearer's sex, social status, and ethnic origin.

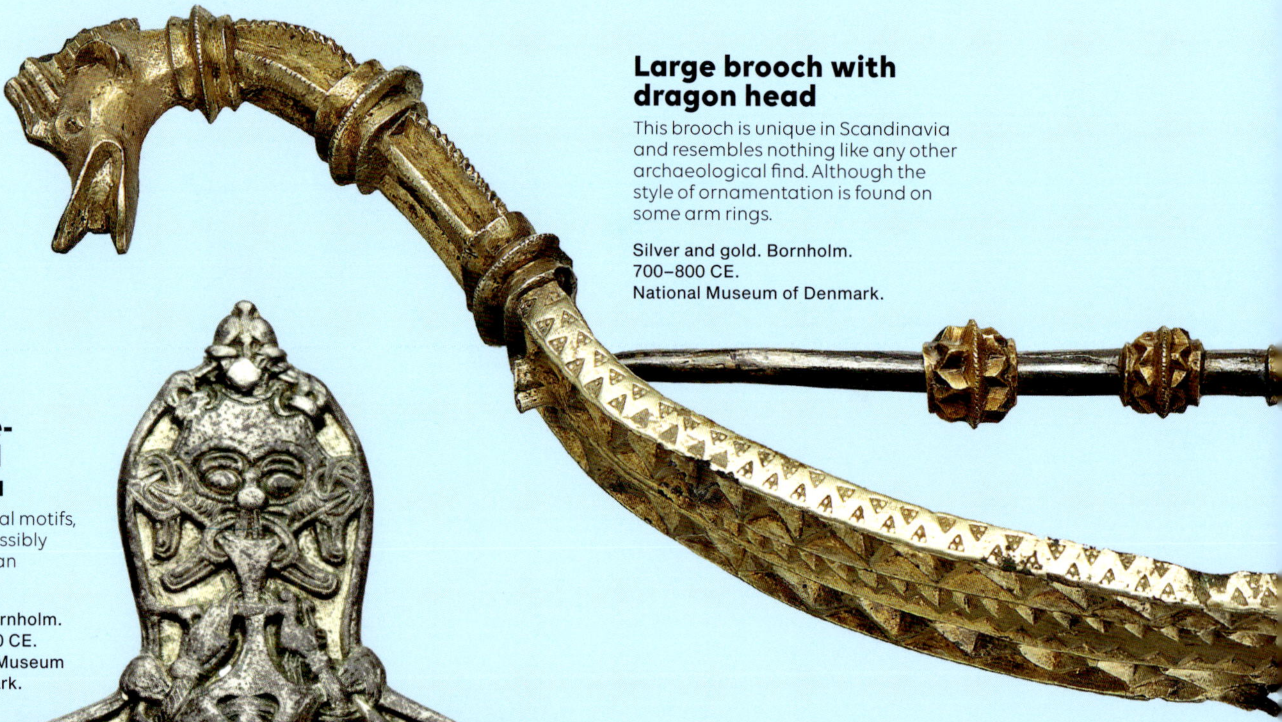

Large brooch with dragon head

This brooch is unique in Scandinavia and resembles nothing like any other archaeological find. Although the style of ornamentation is found on some arm rings.

Silver and gold. Bornholm.
700–800 CE.
National Museum of Denmark.

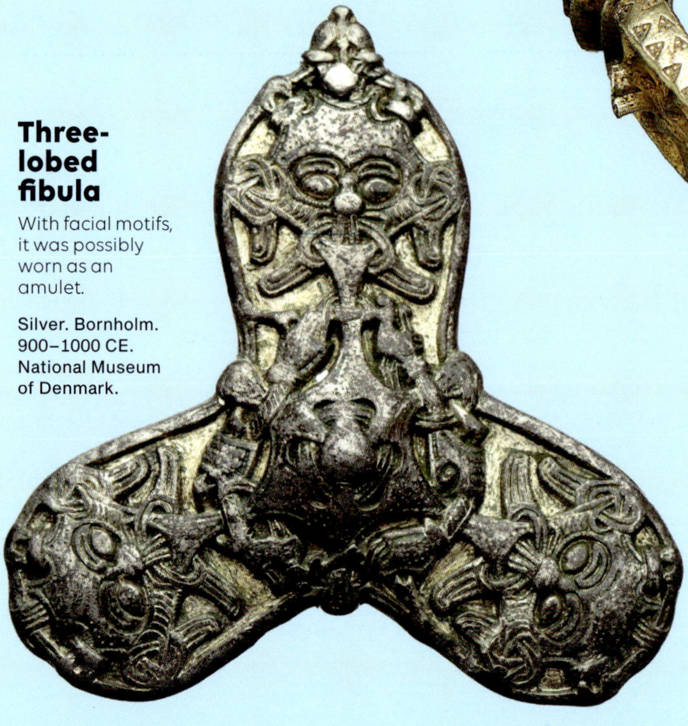

Three-lobed fibula

With facial motifs, it was possibly worn as an amulet.

Silver. Bornholm.
900–1000 CE.
National Museum of Denmark.

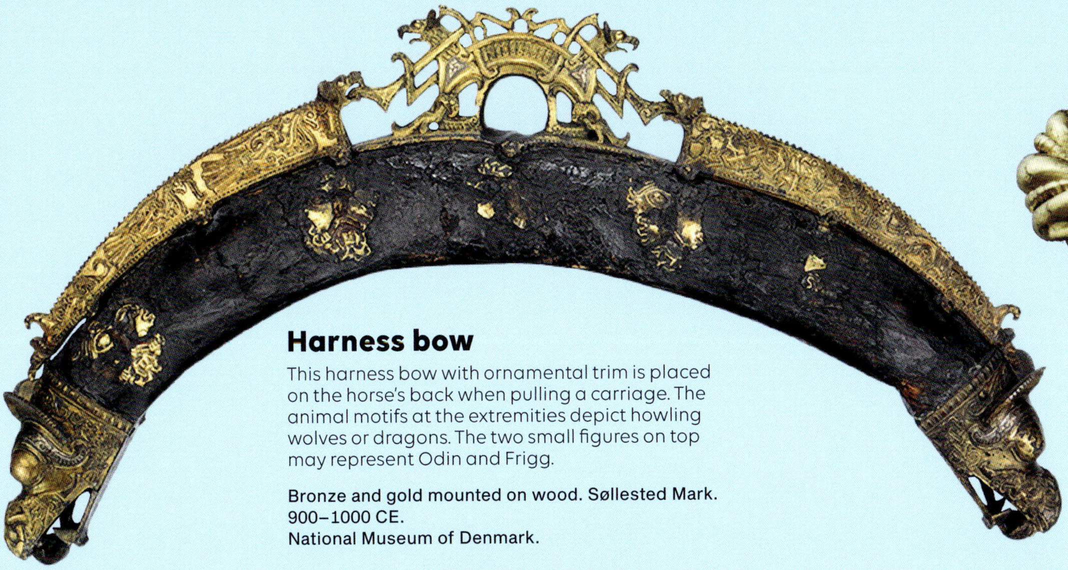

Harness bow

This harness bow with ornamental trim is placed on the horse's back when pulling a carriage. The animal motifs at the extremities depict howling wolves or dragons. The two small figures on top may represent Odin and Frigg.

Bronze and gold mounted on wood. Søllested Mark.
900–1000 CE.
National Museum of Denmark.

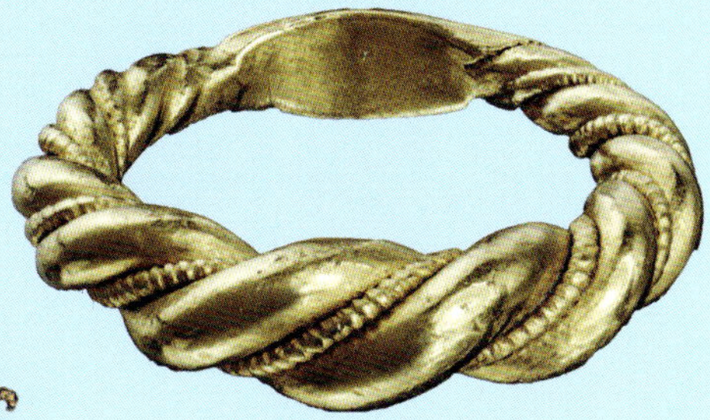

Gold finger ring

Bornholm.
National Museum of Denmark.

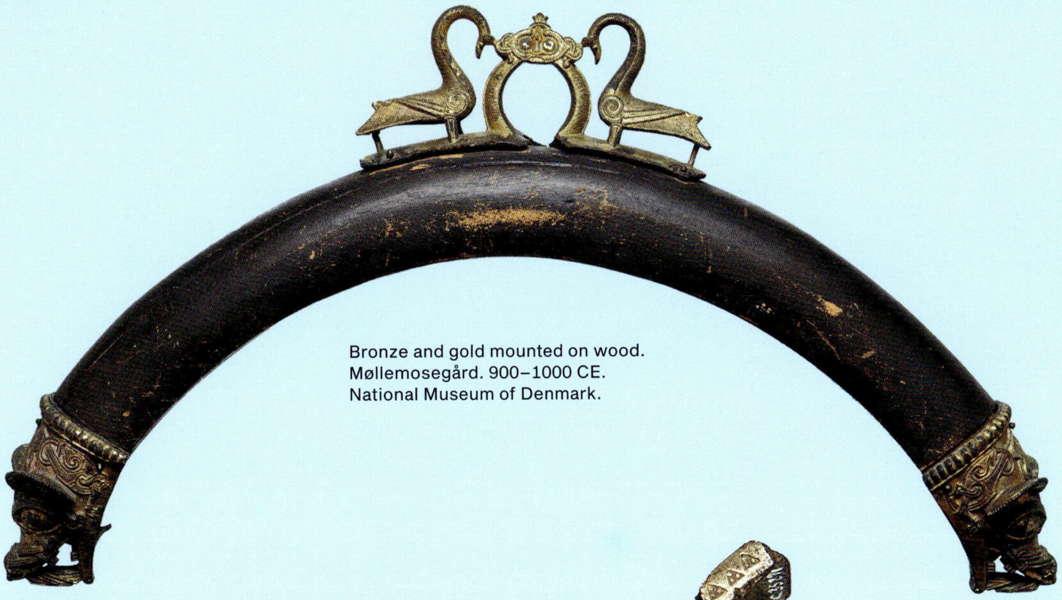

Bronze and gold mounted on wood.
Møllemosegård. 900–1000 CE.
National Museum of Denmark.

Fibula

The Urnes Style represents the last animal style of the Viking Age. It takes its name from sculpted wood panels on a church in the village of Urnes. This asymmetrical style often features a single motif that covers the entire surface. Slender hare-like creatures battle snakes in dynamic, swirling motifs. It appeared in the mid-11th century and dominated the 12th century. This fibula is typical of the Urnes Style. It depicts the extent of the Vikings' trade routes and marks the end of the Viking Age.

Silver, bronze.
Hasseris. 1040–1100 CE.
National Museum of Denmark.

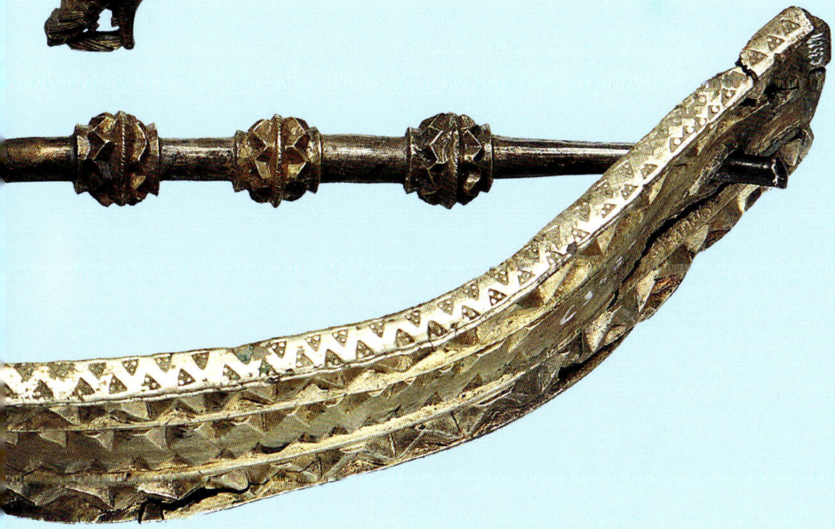

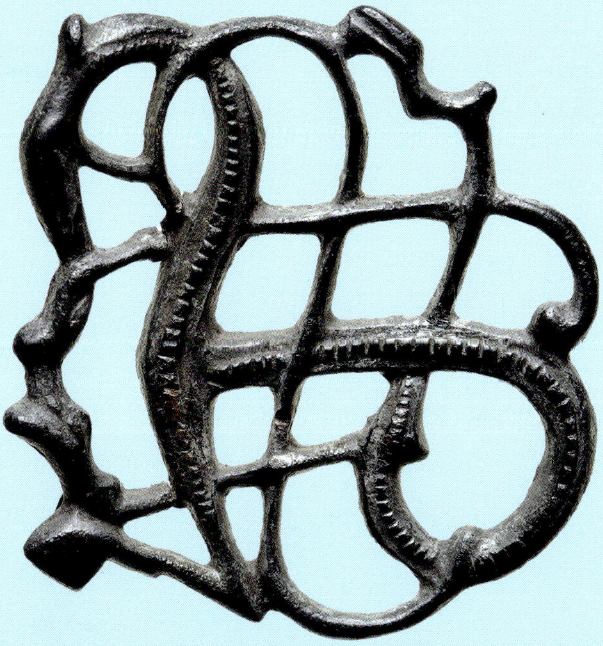

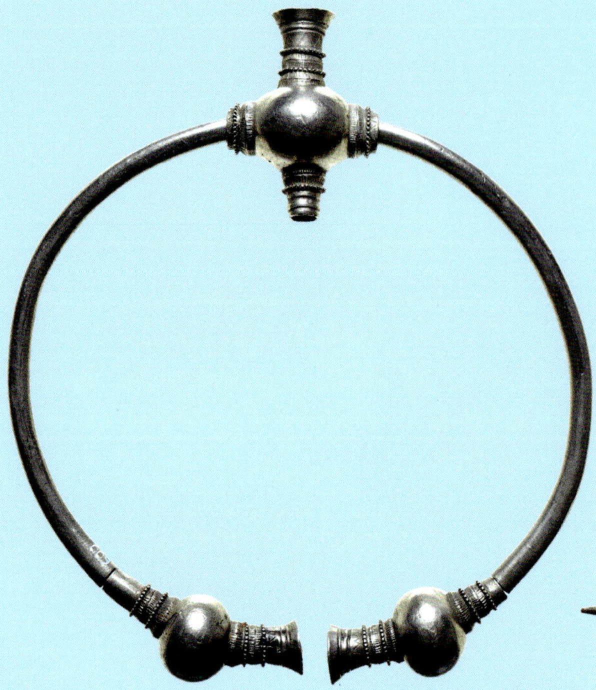

Penannular brooch

Left, penannular brooch (pin missing) with ball-shaped terminals.

Silver. Frederiksborg. 900–1000 CE.
National Museum of Denmark.

Right, penannular brooch with ball-shaped terminals.

Silver.
National Museum of Denmark.

Bottom, ring pin of bronze with gripping beast ornamentation.

Bronze. Sweden. 850–950 CE.
National Museum of Denmark.

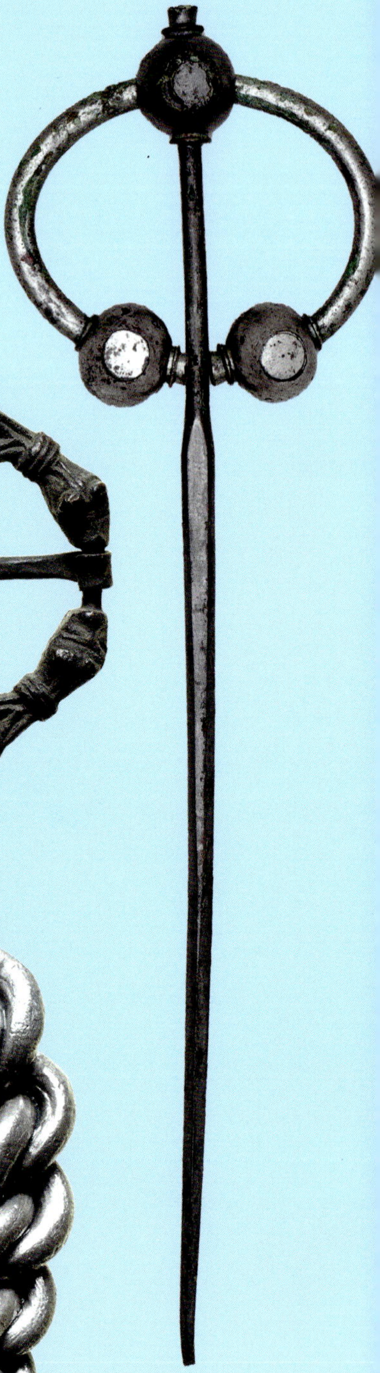

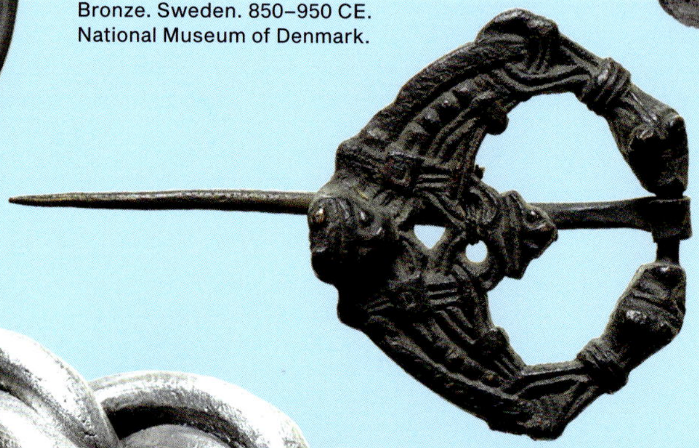

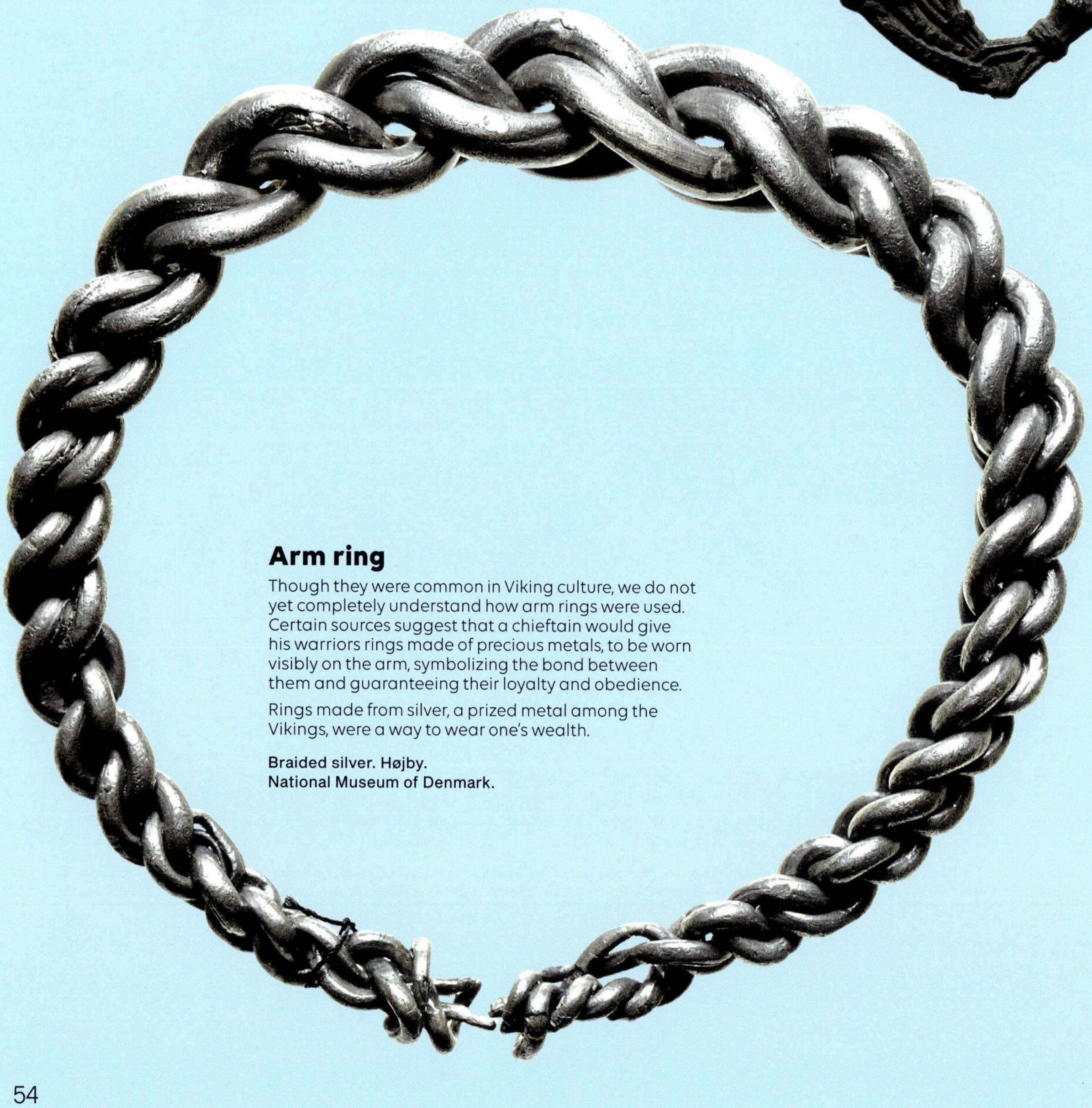

Arm ring

Though they were common in Viking culture, we do not yet completely understand how arm rings were used. Certain sources suggest that a chieftain would give his warriors rings made of precious metals, to be worn visibly on the arm, symbolizing the bond between them and guaranteeing their loyalty and obedience.

Rings made from silver, a prized metal among the Vikings, were a way to wear one's wealth.

Braided silver. Højby.
National Museum of Denmark.

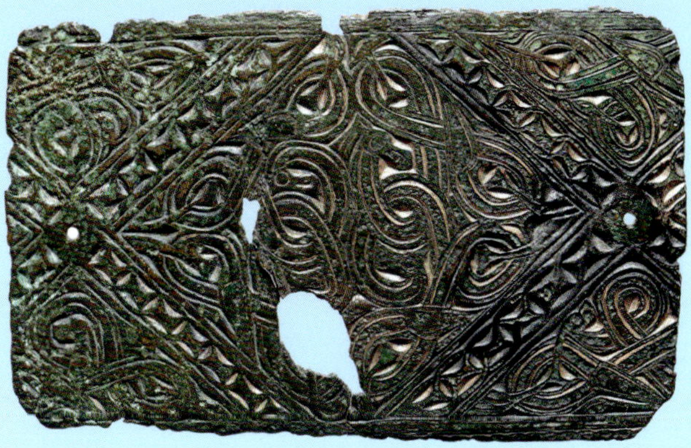

Brooch

Bronze. Svejstrup. 725–800 CE.
National Museum of Denmark.

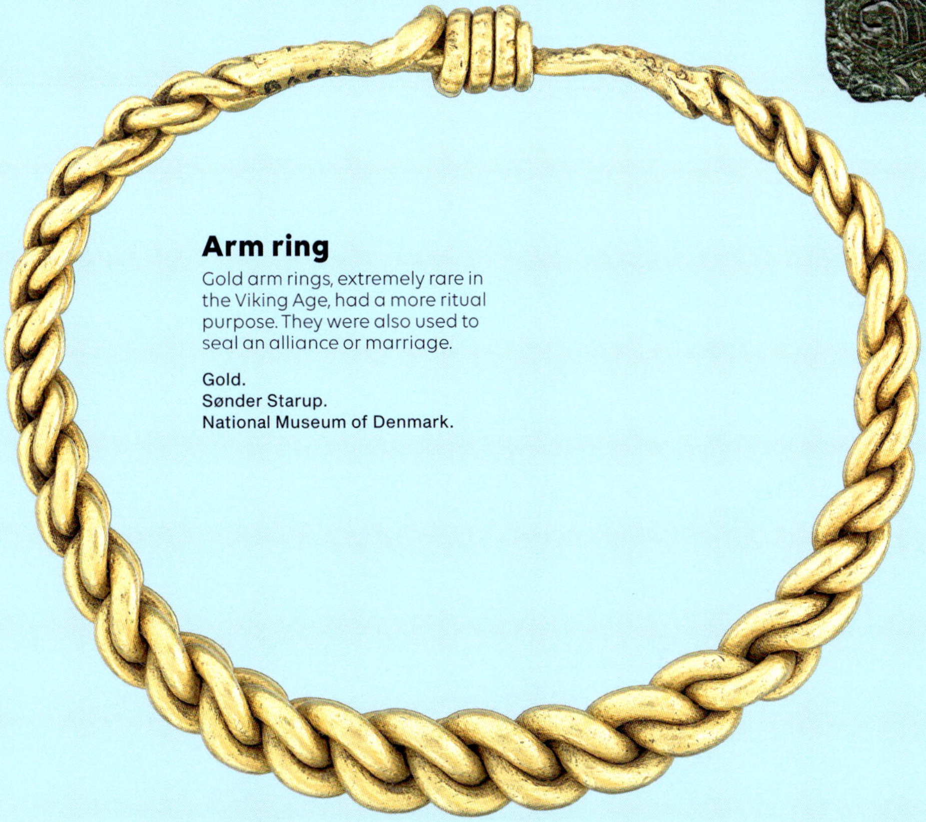

Arm ring

Gold arm rings, extremely rare in the Viking Age, had a more ritual purpose. They were also used to seal an alliance or marriage.

Gold.
Sønder Starup.
National Museum of Denmark.

Silver. Ketting. 875–925 CE.
National Museum of Denmark.

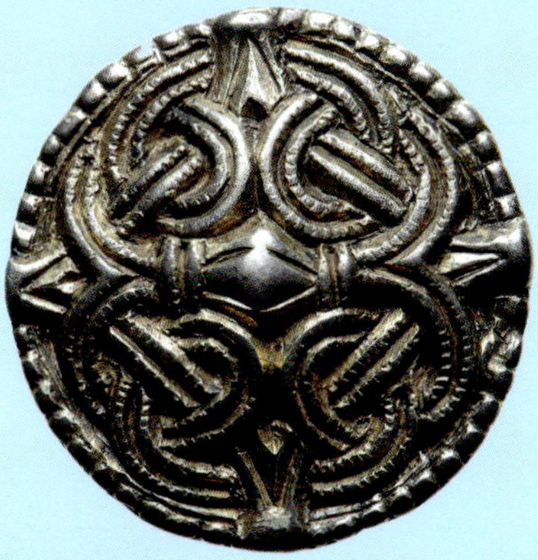

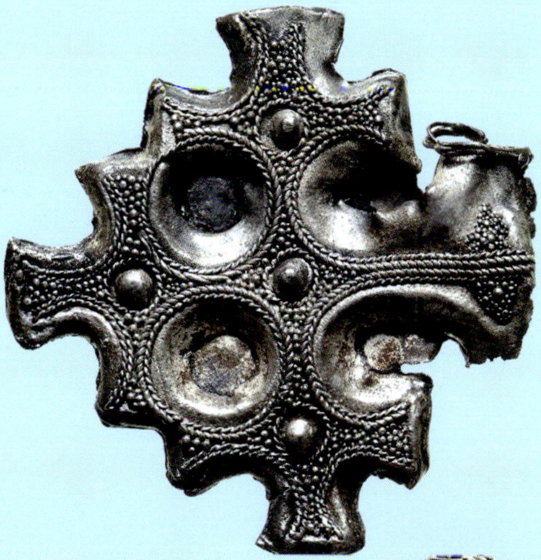

Silver beads and cross-shaped pendant

This motif comes from the Baltic region.

Silver. Randers.
925–975 CE.
National Museum of Denmark.

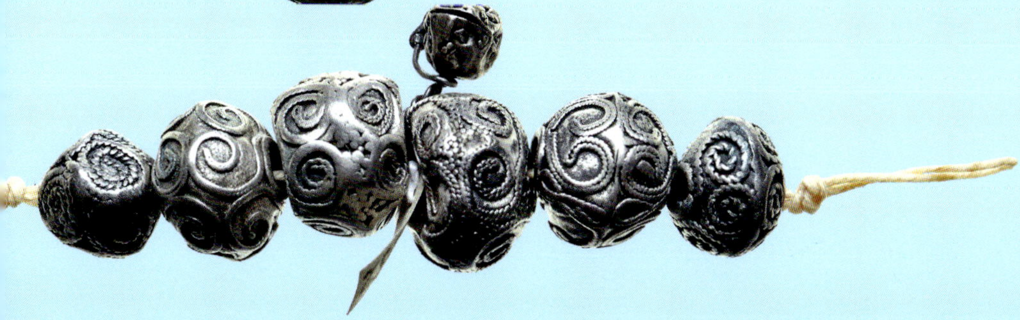

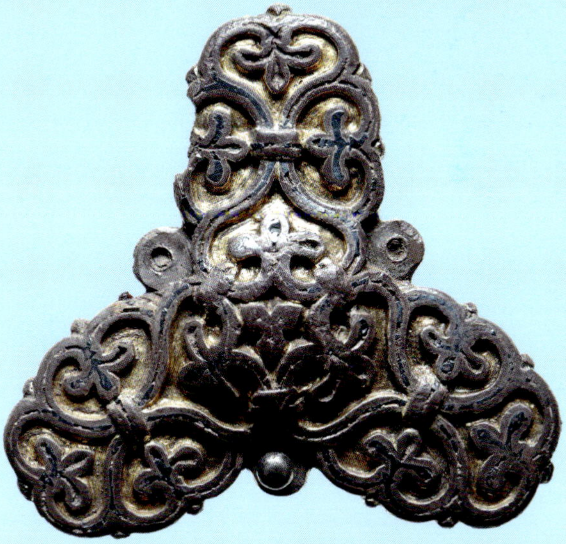

Frankish trefoil-shaped baldric mount

The Vikings were fond of glitz. They wore quantities of mass-produced jewellery, which is why archaeologists find so many brooches at dig sites.

Gilded silver with niello. Borbjerg.
800–950 CE.
National Museum of Denmark.

Saga of the End of Time

"Then shall the sea surge forth over the land, the Midgard Serpent stirring in its giant wrath. It shall spit venom, forming whirlwinds in air and water, a hideous sight. Then shall Thor slay the Midgard Serpent and stride away nine paces before falling dead because of the venom that the serpent has spit on him. Then shall Surtr cast fire over the earth and burn all the world."

Excerpt from the *Prose Edda*.

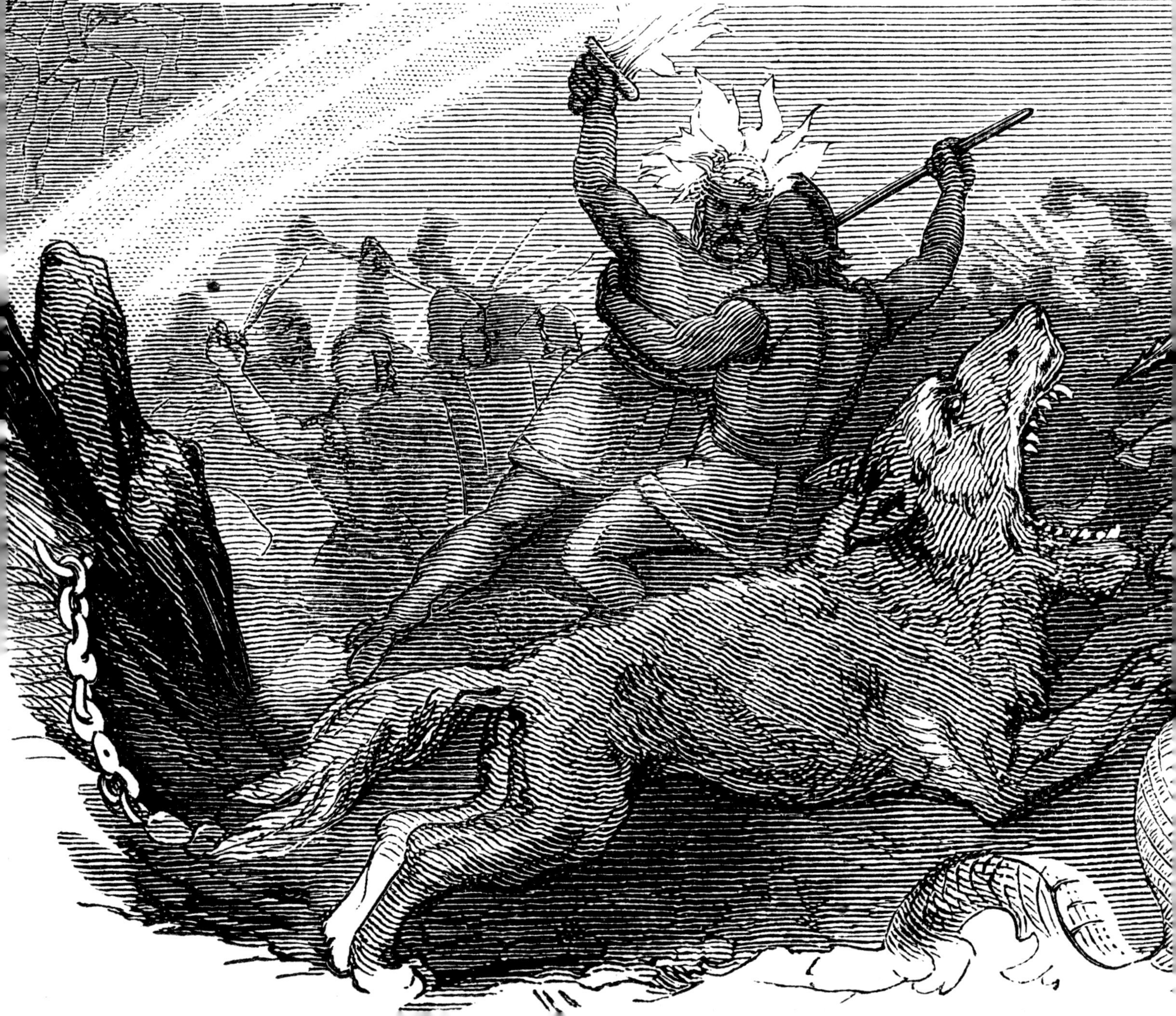

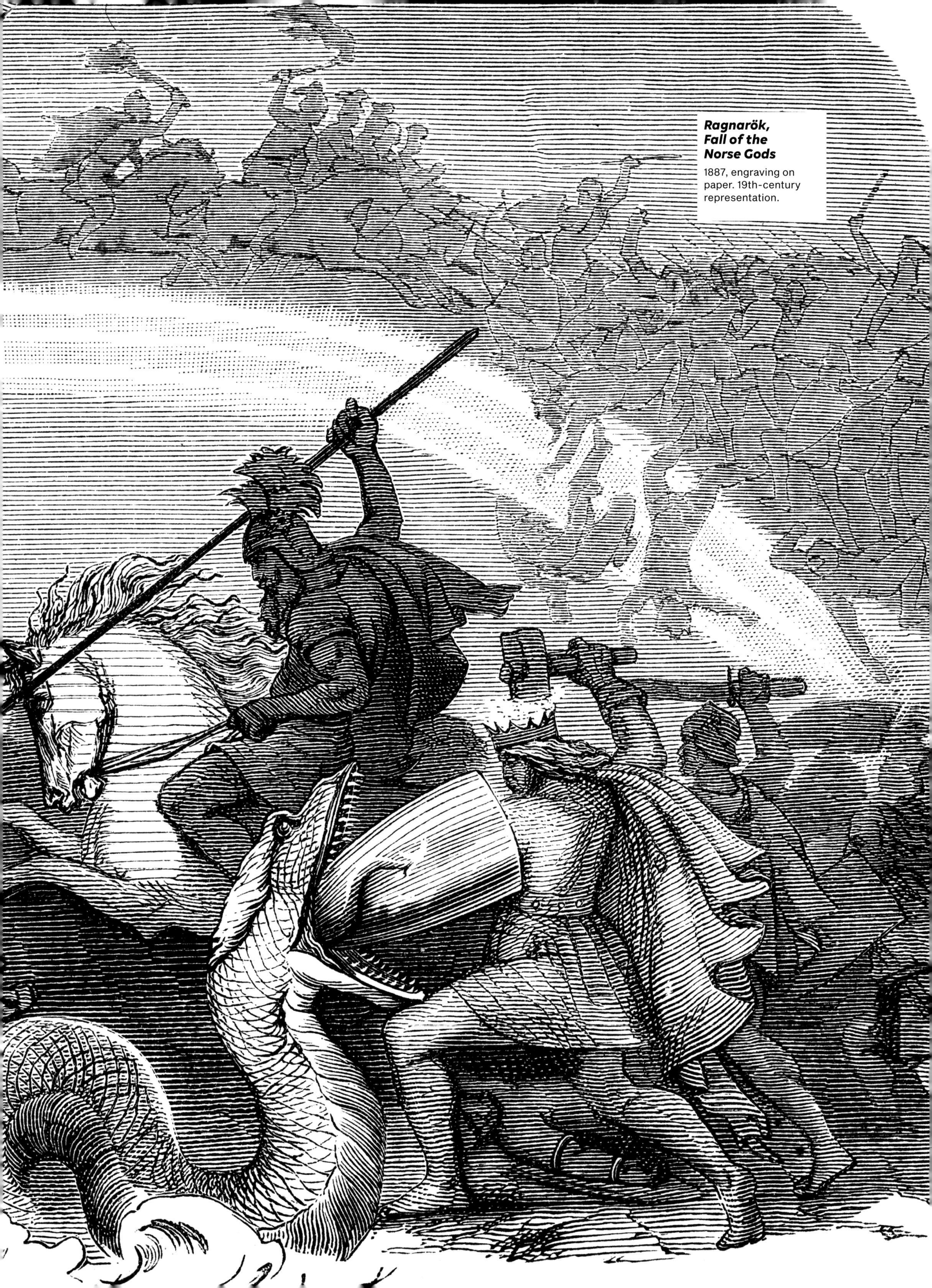

Ragnarök, Fall of the Norse Gods

1887, engraving on paper. 19th-century representation.

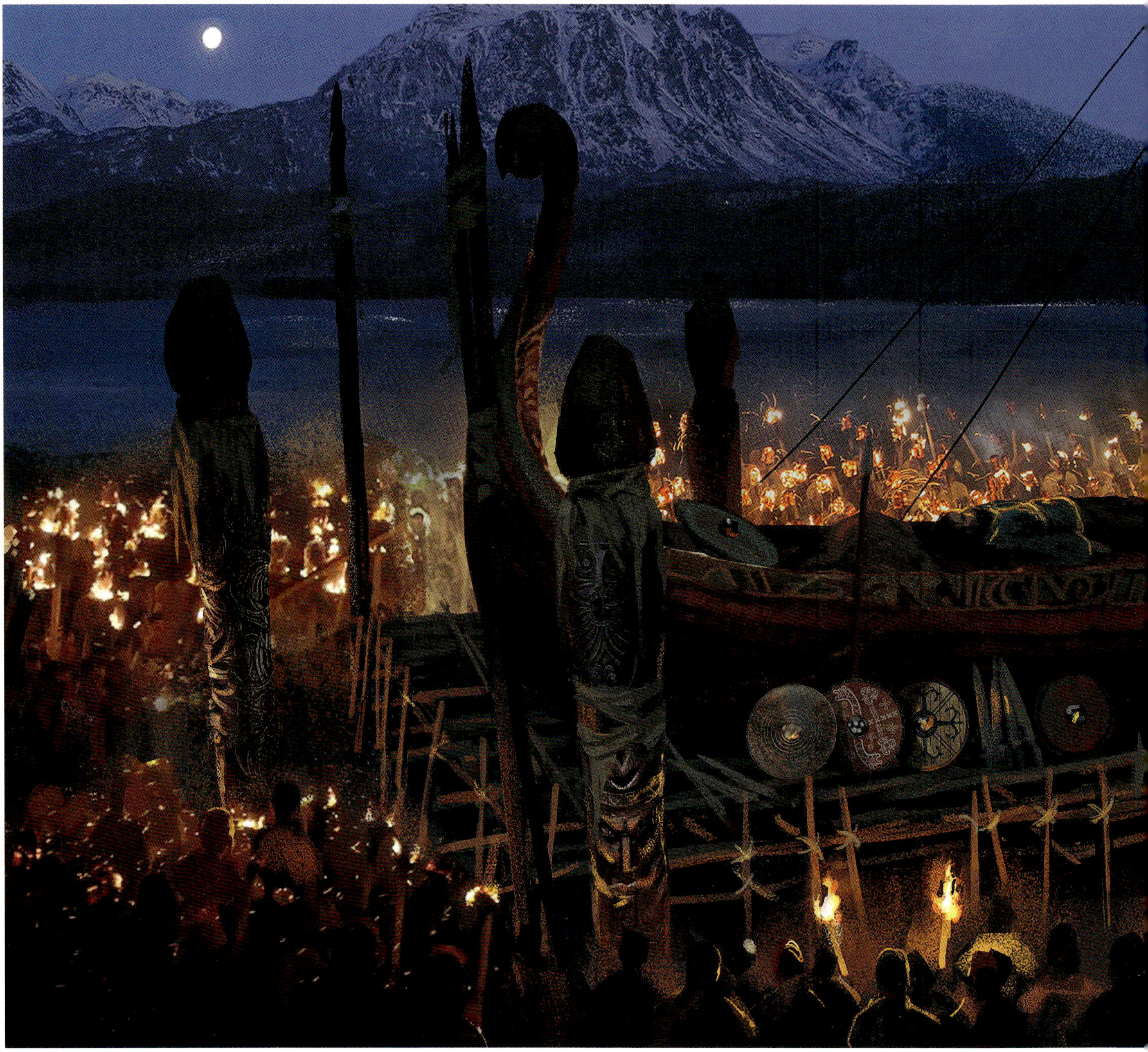

Dead and undead

Living among the dead

Peter Pentz, curator at the National Museum of Denmark

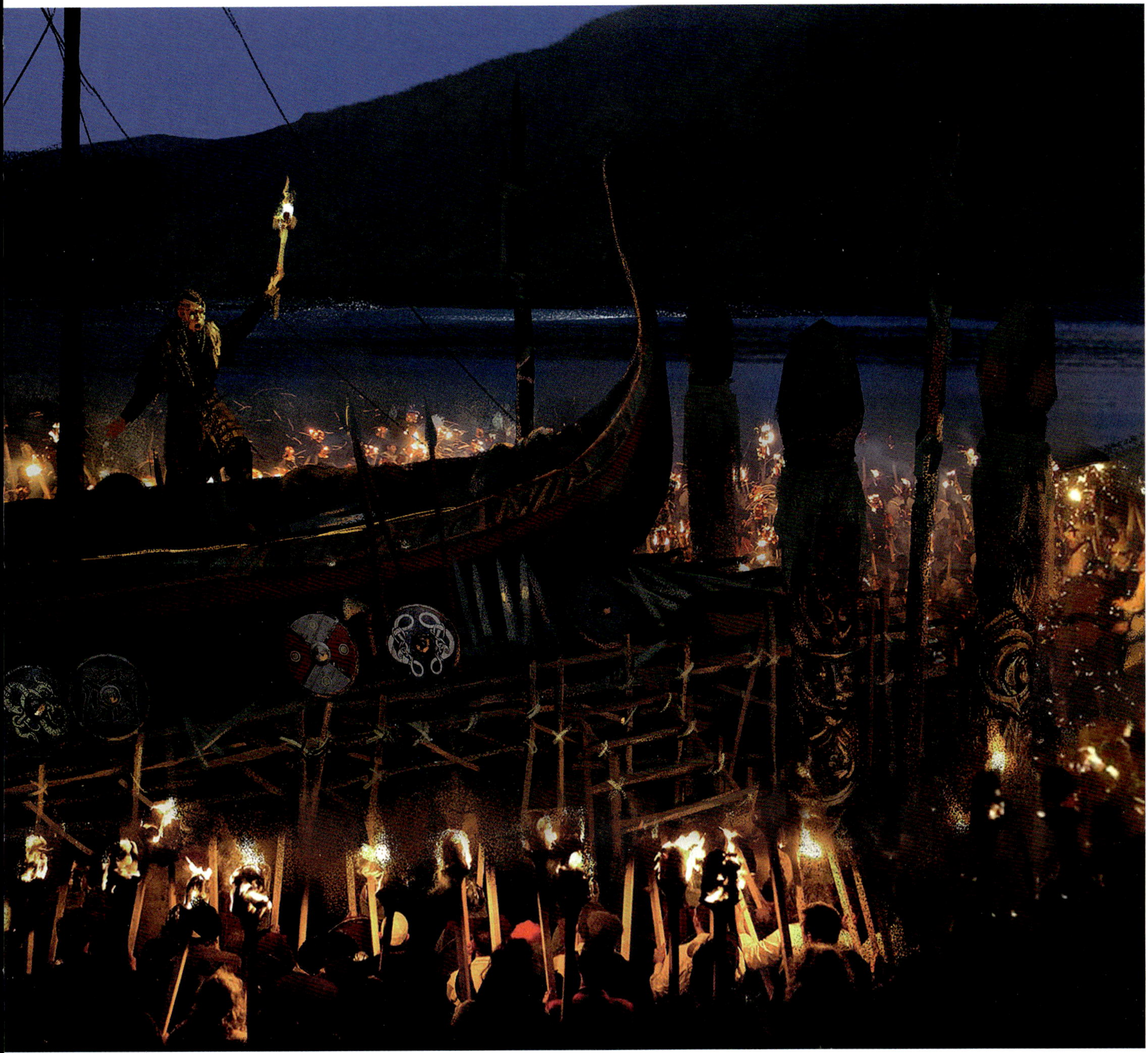

The Vikings did not seem to regard death as permanent, but more as a transition from one state to another. Ghosts could cross the boundaries between these states. The Vikings also lived amongst their dead—they were visibly commemorated in burial mounds and sometimes even remembered with an inscription on a runestone.

Because people's memories lived on, the ways in which they died had much significance. The best death was on the battlefield. The most wretched was to die quietly in the sickbed.

The Vikings had no concept of people having souls. They did, however, believe that they had followers in life that could give advice and that were an expression of their character. The followers could be animals, but they could also be female ancestors that came in a dream, predicted your destiny and guided you through life.

It is the dead Vikings who tell us about the living. Thousands of graves from the Viking Age have been excavated, the graves of women and men, children, people at the peak of their life, the elderly and the ancient.

ABOVE

Art by Guang Yu Tan.

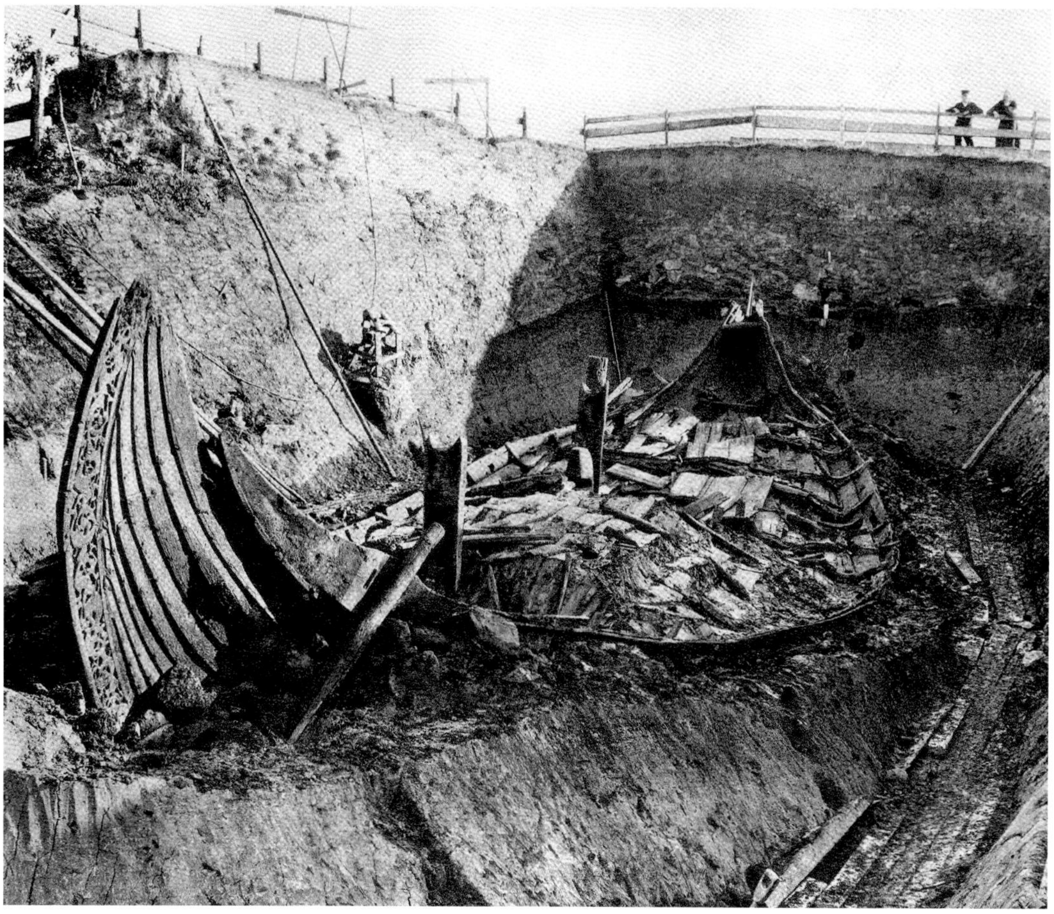

ABOVE
Burial ship in Oseberg, Norway, undergoing archaeological excavation, 1904.

FACING PAGE
Some wealthy Viking graves were marked with slabs or stones arranged in the form of a ship, perhaps meant to transport the deceased to the afterlife. The Jelling Stone Ship, some 170 metres long, is the largest known funeral ship. It is also among the most ancient Viking Age monuments at Jelling.

Burying the dead was done in many ways. Many were cremated, others were not. Some were buried with many gifts, others with nothing. Many probably didn't even receive a burial. The Vikings grave monuments, burial mounds, stone ships and runestones are the oldest surviving evidence of that period's conceptual universes. Throughout the whole of Scandinavia and other areas where Vikings settled, monuments in the landscape stand as a reminder of their presence and thoughts. In the Vikings' own time, the grave monuments spread out, or clustered together in the landscape, represented an actual dead-world, a visible reminder of the deceased. It was a world shared by the living and dead, or rather, the undead.

Graves can also tell us about status. The status a person held in Viking society, followed them to the grave. Large ship burials with sacrificed animals and people and other grave goods are the epitaphs left behind by kings and chiefs. The affluent classes received simpler, but still elaborate burials, in burial chambers, wagons and coffins. The lower classes and enslaved people had little status in Viking society, nor were they recognised with a magnificent burial.

Vikings and Christ

The shift to Christianity was one of the greatest upheavals in Scandinavian history. Inscribed on a great runestone in Jelling, Denmark, which was raised in 965, is the declaration of king Harald Bluetooth that he has converted the Danes to Christianity. They are strong words and they make up just a short sentence of the long tale about changing religions.

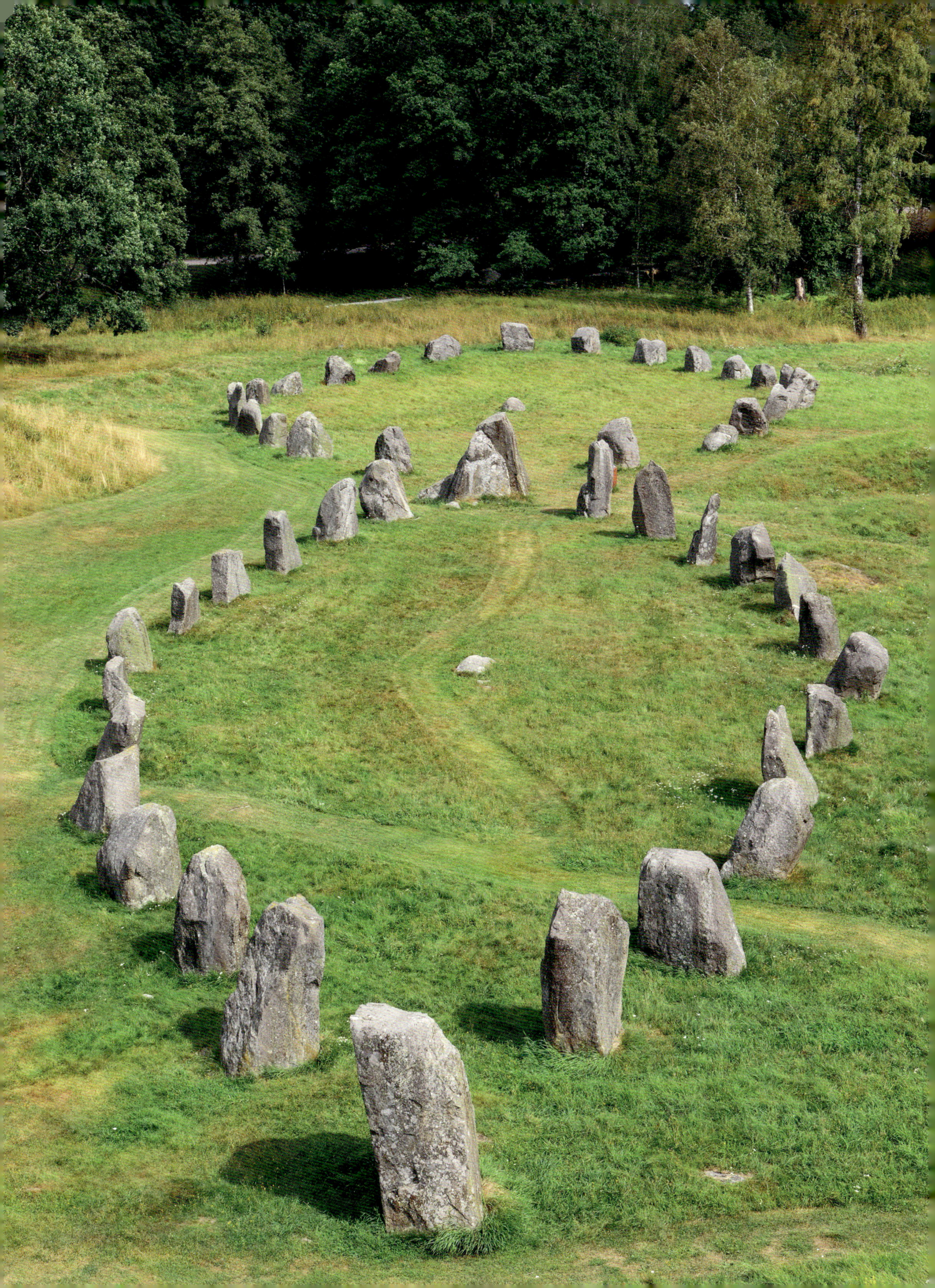

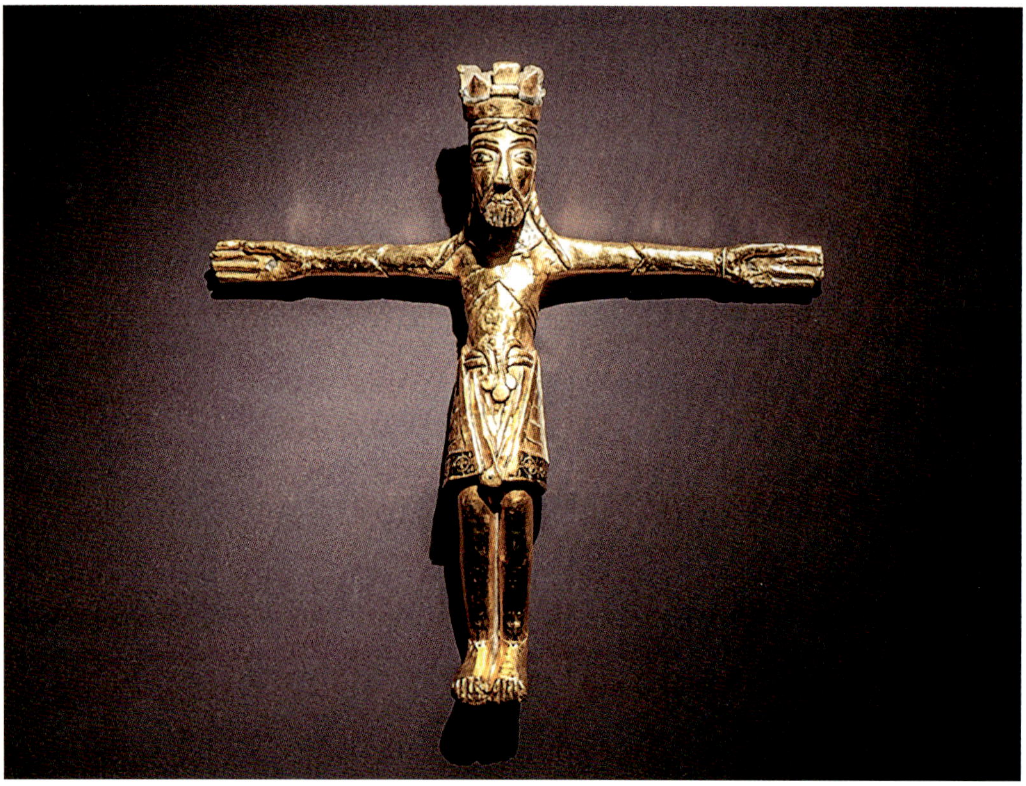

Åby Crucifix

Almost 1,000 years old, the Åby crucifix depicts Christ as a triumphant warrior king, eyes open, wearing a Viking mustache, noble clothing, and a crown. In the Viking spirit, the supreme god is a god of war.

Copper. Reconstitution. National Museum of Denmark.

If you believe the written accounts, then Christianity came to Denmark from abroad, brought either by devout and fearless missionaries, or by victorious kings who baptised the defeated Norsemen by force. Archaeologists give a more nuanced picture of the upheaval, primarily from the study of graves and the way the Vikings buried their dead.

Burials reflect the society the deceased lived in—his or her conceptual universe and identity. Articles, from obviously Christian contexts, have been found in graves from the 8th century—long before the start of the Viking Age and any known Christian mission in Scandinavia. Articles such as Byzantine silver spoons, that were used in late roman churches, or coins with Christian symbols. This information cannot tell us anything definite about the faith of the deceased but can help us to learn about their identity and the society they lived in. It does tell us that Norsemen had known about Christianity for centuries.

A tale about how the missionaries came to Birka—the large Viking market town in Sweden—recounts how the missionaries met a Christian society that had existed since antiquity. These kinds of communities were very influential in the religious upheaval. Even though Harald Bluetooth and the missionaries would like to have been responsible for introducing Christianity, they hardly deserve all the credit.

It was through interactions with others, like the market town communities, that Viking Christianity emerged. The goal for missionaries was not only to convert the Vikings, but also to regulate and adapt what had already been formed through meeting between Christian and Norsemen.

Viking Age artisans and their first Christian artworks originated from this mixed culture. The Jelling stone carvings are a wonderful blend of the Vikings' animal images and Christian art. A small, gilded silver goblet found in the enormous north mound at Jelling is also a hybrid—in shape as well as ornamentation. ▮

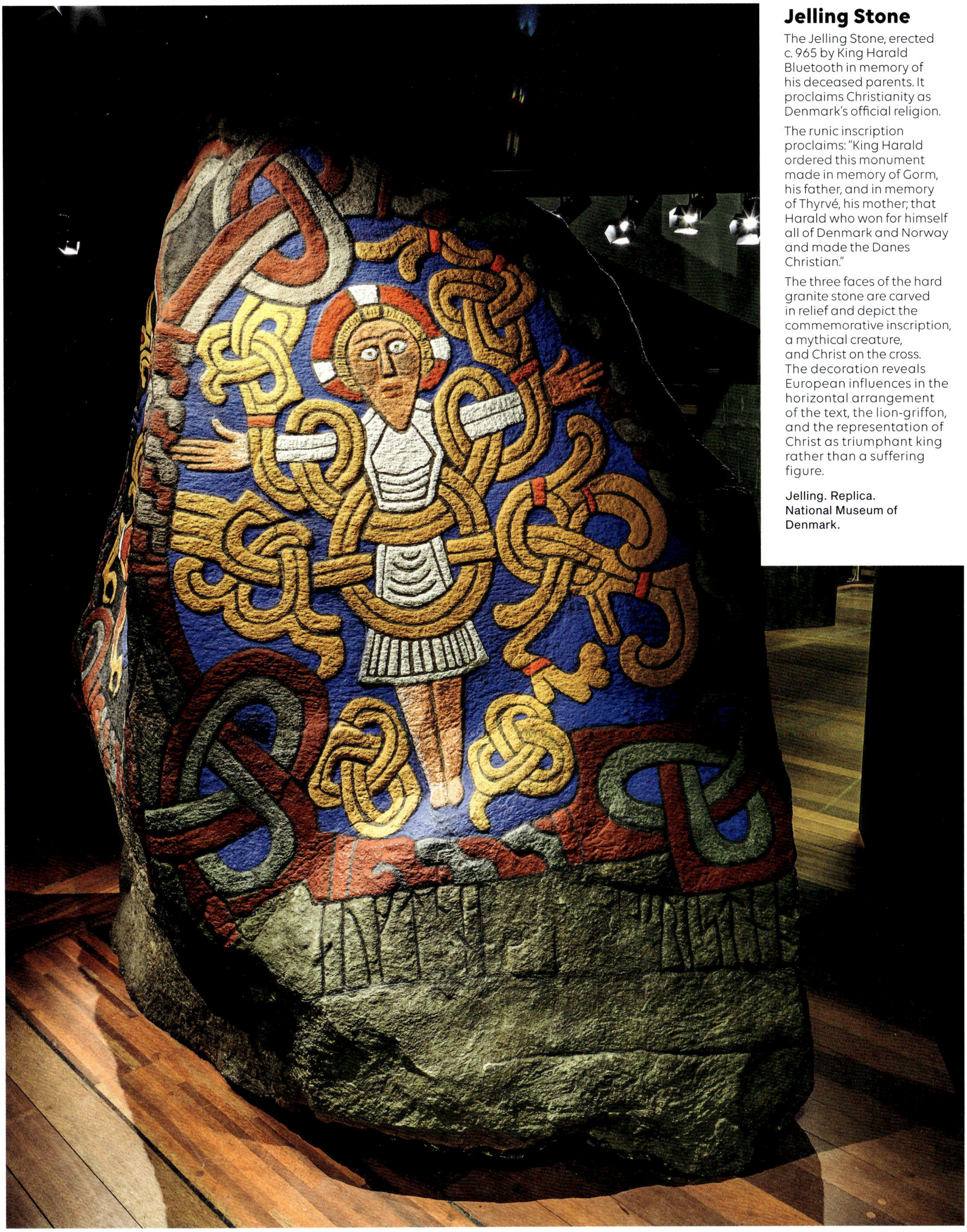

Jelling Stone

The Jelling Stone, erected c. 965 by King Harald Bluetooth in memory of his deceased parents. It proclaims Christianity as Denmark's official religion.

The runic inscription proclaims: "King Harald ordered this monument made in memory of Gorm, his father, and in memory of Thyrvé, his mother; that Harald who won for himself all of Denmark and Norway and made the Danes Christian."

The three faces of the hard granite stone are carved in relief and depict the commemorative inscription, a mythical creature, and Christ on the cross. The decoration reveals European influences in the horizontal arrangement of the text, the lion-griffon, and the representation of Christ as triumphant king rather than a suffering figure.

Jelling. Replica. National Museum of Denmark.

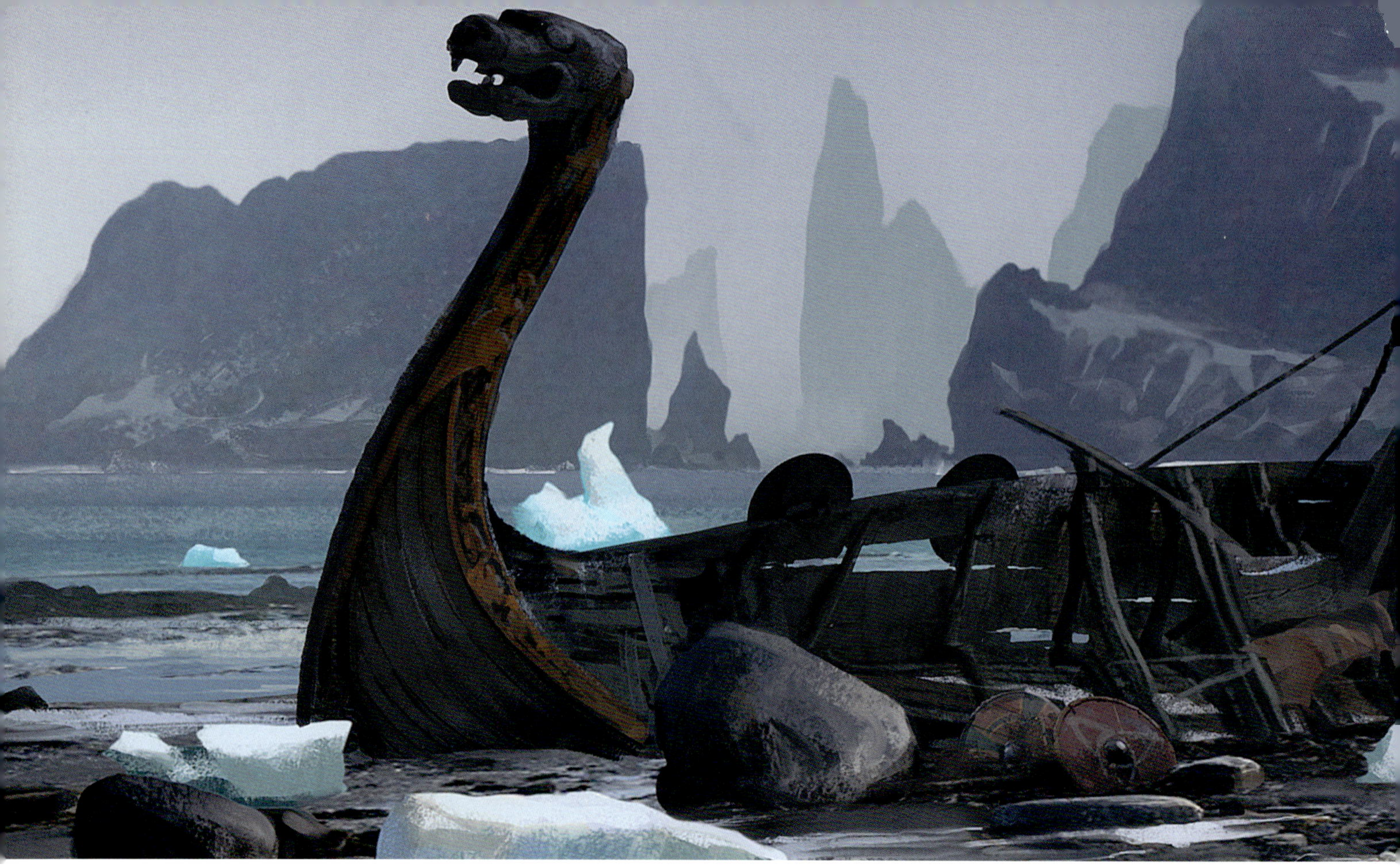

Endgame

THE END OF THE VIKING AGE

Claude Pommereau

October 1066. The Anglo-Saxons are defeated by the Normans of William the Conqueror at Hastings. This event, along with the Battle of Stamford Bridge, marks the end of the Viking Age. But looking past this chronological marker set by historians, several factors contributed to the disappearance of the Viking way of life: the arrival of Christianity, the unification of Scandinavian kingdoms, trade competition, and the Vikings' rapid assimilation into the lands they colonized.

The Norse were among the Western peoples most reluctant to adopt Christianity. Farmers and warriors were attached to their ancestral beliefs. Ultimately, their gradual and belated adhesion to Christianity was related to their conquests in Christian lands; it being difficult to bring altars and representations of gods with them on expeditions, the Vikings were often without their familiar religious framework. They were rarely accompanied by wives and settled down in the areas they conquered. Rollo is a highly symbolic example. Having settled near Rouen, he converted to Christianity and, in doing so, lost his taste for plunder, finding the idea of robbing monasteries in Frankish lands distasteful.

The Vikings were above all traders. To conduct their business, they had to negotiate with inhabitants of the Eastern plains or Western realms, all of whom were Christian. Viking chieftains founded kingdoms in lands whose populations were mostly evangelized, and they found common understanding with bishops. In Scandinavia itself, evangelization began in the 10th century. Missionaries sent to Norse lands soon discovered that these earthly peoples were indifferent to their message and that they would have to work

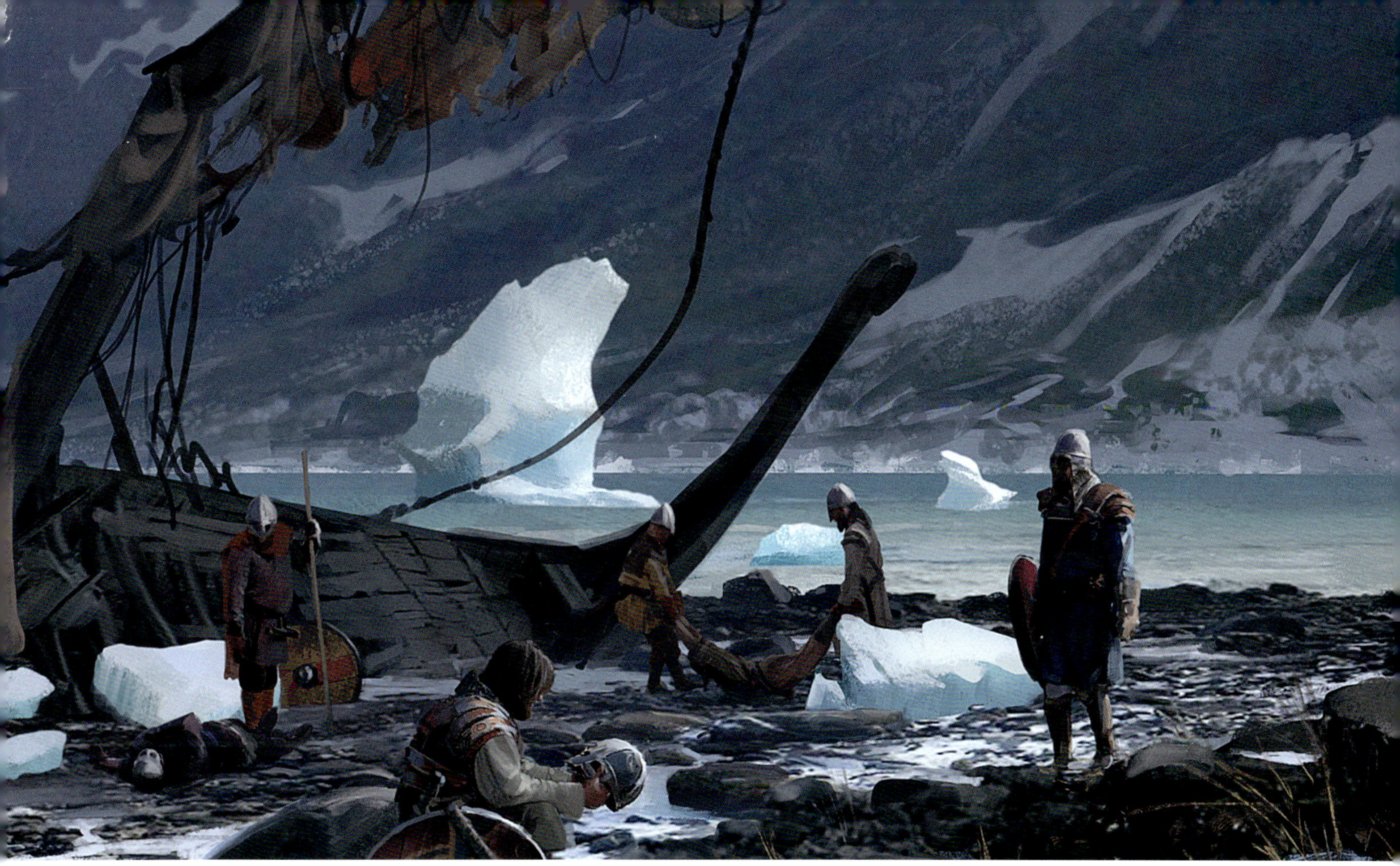

through their rulers. The tactic paid off quickly in Denmark. In Norway, King Haakon the Good, recently returned from England, where he had been baptized, argued for the adoption of Christianity before the Thing, the assembly of nobles and freemen.

In Sweden, it proved even more delicate, with the old beliefs persisting into the 11th century, so one had to deal with the local gods. In the East, the Varangians, Swedish Vikings who founded Kyiv (the capital of Ukraine), were forced to convert along with the Slavs in 989 during the mass baptism ordered by King Vladimir I. The conversion to Christianity ended the slave trade and introduced a church that was opposed to raids.

Viking chieftains also encountered powerful kings in Europe, ruling stable hereditary monarchies. And Christianity exposed the Vikings to the enticing notion of royalty by divine right. It was an astonishing concept for these formidable warriors—for two centuries, no son of a Norse king had ever succeeded his father. Viking chieftains, normally quite happy to kill one another, were replaced by powerful barons concerned with political stability, though the very notion of belonging to a nation had only arisen in the 10th century. As raiders, the Vikings had had little interest in identifying as Swedish, Danish, or Norwegian. The emergence of nationality thus sounded another death knell for the Viking way of life.

In addition, the Vikings adapted to the lands they settled with astonishing ease. Recognized as masters of Normandy in 911, by 950, most had adopted the Frankish language. In England, when William the Conqueror arrived in 1066, they were already assimilated into the Anglo-Saxon way of life. In Russia and Kyiv, their adoption of Slavic customs was just as impressive..

One last reason for their disappearance was that by the 11th century, trade had changed. The transport of raw materials necessitated heavy ships. Viking vessels were perfect for plundering lightweight items of value such as jewels or coins, but those days were over, and the Viking's highly specialized ships were no longer useful. A Viking without a ship was like a rider without a horse. The end of the Viking way of life was just a matter of time. ▮

ABOVE

Art by Martin Deschambault.

Assassin's Creed® Valhalla – TM&Copyright © Ubisoft Entertainment.

VIKINGS
Dragons of the Northern Sea

April 14 to Octobre 10, 2022

Plan your visit

Pointe-à-Callière, Montréal Archaelogy and History Complex
350 Place Royale
Old Montréal (Québec) Canada H2Y 3Y5
Mail: info@pacmusee.qc.ca – Tel: 514 872-9150 – pacmusee.qc.ca

Anne Élisabeth Thibault, Executive Director
Christine Dufresne, Director Exhibitions-Multimedias Technologies
Samuel Moreau, Project Manager – Exhibitions

How to get to the Museum
Metro: Place-d'Armes Station
Bus: 715, from metro Berri-UQAM or Peel

This exhibition is produced by Pointe-à-Callière, Montréal Archaeology and History Complex, in partnership with the National Museum of Denmark and MuseumsPartner, Austria. In collaboration with Ubisoft Montréal.

Montréal

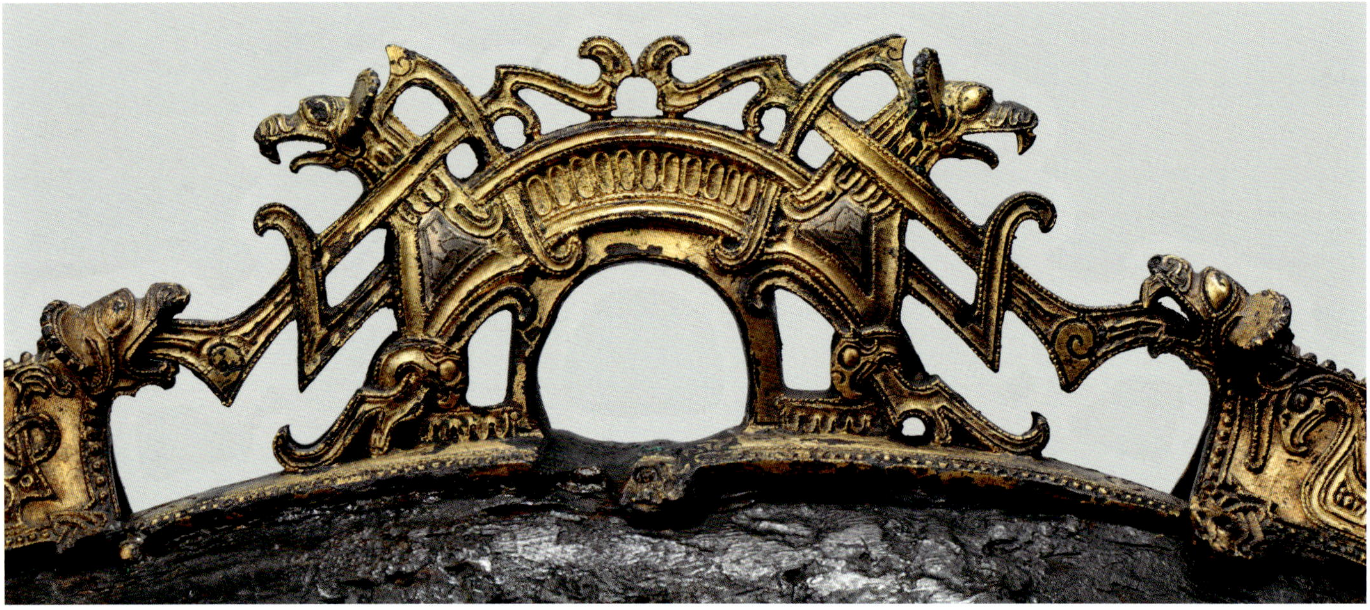

Harness bow (detail).
Bronze and gold mounted on wood.
Søllested Mark. 900–1000 CE.
National Museum of Denmark.

BeauxArts &Cie

A publication by **Beaux Arts & Cie**
9, boulevard de la Madeleine
75038 Paris Cedex 1
Tél. + 33187899100 – Fax 0187899149
www.beauxarts.com
RCS Paris B 435 355 896

Editor **Claude Pommereau**
Graphic Design **Marguerite Da Silva**
Iconographer **Pierre Morio**
Editorial assistant **Capucine Jahan**
Translator **Peter Christensen**

Collaboration for this issue
Marc Carrier, Michèle Hayeur Smith, Dominique de La Tour, Peter Pentz, Christine Tremblay Corneau, Birgitta Wallace

Beaux Arts & Cie
President **Frédéric Jousset**
Managing Director **Solenne Blanc**
Assistant Director
Jean-Baptiste Costa de Beauregard
Director of Partnerships and
Assistant Publications Director **Marion de Flers**
Art Director **Bernard Borel**

Editorial Manager **Solène de Bure**
Partnerships and Publications
Project Coordinator **Charlotte Ullmann**
Product Manager **Léa Schiavo**

ISBN **979-1-020407320**
Copyright Deposit **March, 2022**
Photoengraving **Key Graphic**, Paris
Printed in France

Bookstore Distribution
Clients UD / Flammarion Diffusion
commandesclients@union-distribution.fr
Tél. + 33141802020

Other Bookstores
Florence Hanappe / Amélie Fontaine
Tél. + 33187899106/04

Sales by correspondance
Beaux Arts magazine
4, rue de Mouchy – 60438 Noailles Cedex
Tél. + 33155567072
abo.beauxarts@groupe-gli.com

Photographic Credits

Cover and P.67: © Pointe-à-Callière/Dominique Boudrias
P.2 et 3: © Nationalmuseum, Copenhague/Photo Soren Greve. P.4-5: © Ubisoft Entertainment™. P.6-7: © Bridgeman images. P.8: © The History Collection/Alamy/Hemis. P.9: © Bridgeman images. P.10: © Royal Library, Copenhague; © Bridgeman images. P.11: © Bridgeman images; © Photo Werner Forman/UIG/Bridgeman images. P.12: Photo D.R. P.13: © Bridgeman images; © Look and learn/Bridgeman images; Photo D.R.; Photo D.R.; Photo D.R.; Photo D.R. P.15: © Ubisoft Entertainment™. P.16: © Pointe-à-Callière/Nicolas Demers. P.17: © Michal Sikorski/Alamy/Hemis; © Stéphane Humbert-Basset. P.18 et 19: © National museum, Copenhague/Photo Soren Greve. P.20: © Bridgeman images; © AKG images; © Bridgeman images. P.21: © Hemis; © Bridgeman images; Photo D.R. P.22-23: © Ubisoft Entertainment™. P.24-25: © Stéphane Humbert-Basset. P.27:© Stefano Bianchetti/Bridgeman Images. P.28: © Photo Grégory Gérault/Hemis; © Nationalmuseum, Copenhague. P.29: © Hemis; © AKG Images; © AKG Images; Photo D.R.; © Bridgeman images; © Bridgeman images; © Hemis; © Bridgeman images; © Bridgeman images. P.30: © Nationalmuseum, Copenhague/Photo John Lee. P.31: © iStock Photo. P.32-33: © Ubisoft Entertainment™. P.33: © Flemming Bau. P.34: © Musée canadien de l'histoire. P.35: © Performance Image/Alamy/Hemis. P.36-37: © Ubisoft Entertainment™. P.38: © Ubisoft Entertainment™. P.39: © Nationalmuseum, Copenhague; © Nationalmuseum, Copenhague/Photo Soren Greve; © Nationalmuseum, Copenhague/Photo Arnold Mikkelsen. P.40: © Historiska museet, Stockholm; © Giancarlo Costa/Bridgeman Images. P.41: © Nationalmuseum, Copenhague; © akg-images/Osprey Publishing/Gerry Embleton. P.42-43: © Ubisoft Entertainment™. P.44-45: © Ubisoft Entertainment™. P.46: © Ubisoft Entertainment™. P.47: © Pointe-à-Callière, Montréal. P.48: © Nationalmuseum, Copenhague/Photo Soren Greve; © Nationalmuseum, Copenhague/Photo John Lee; © Nationalmuseum, Copenhague/Photo Soren Greve. p.49: © Photo Aurélien Brusini/Hemis. P.50: © Flemming Bau. P.51: © Nationalmuseum, Copenhague/Photo Arnold Mikkelsen; © Nationalmuseum, Copenhague/Photo Soren Greve; © Nationalmuseum, Copenhague/Photo Soren Greve; © Nationalmuseum, Copenhague/Photo Jana Trepte. P.52: © Nationalmuseum, Copenhague; © Nationalmuseum, Copenhague/Photo Soren Greve; P.53 : © Nationalmuseum, Copenhague/Photo John Lee; © Nationalmuseum, Copenhague/Photo John Lee; © Nationalmuseum, Copenhague/Photo Soren Greve; © Nationalmuseum, Copenhague/Photo Soren Greve. P.54: © Nationalmuseum, Copenhague/Photo Soren Greve. P.55: © Nationalmuseum, Copenhague/Photo Arnold Mikkelsen; © Nationalmuseum, Copenhague/Photo Soren Greve. P.56-57: © akg-images/Interfoto/Sammlung Rauch. P.58-59: © Ubisoft Entertainment™. P.60: © Kulturhistorisk museum, Oslo. P.61: © Janzig/Europe/Alamy/Hemis. P.62: © Nationalmuseum, Copenhague. P.63: © Nationalmuseum, Copenhague. P.64-65: © Ubisoft Entertainment™. P.66: © Nationalmuseum, Copenhague.